THE MONROE DOCTRINE AND WORLD PEACE

THE MONROE DOCTRINE
AND WORLD PEACE

by
EVARTS SEELYE SCUDDER

KENNIKAT PRESS
Port Washington, N. Y./London

Theodore Lownik Library
Illinois Benedictine College
Lisle, Illinois 60532

327.73
S436m

THE MONROE DOCTRINE AND WORLD PEACE

First published in 1939
Reissued in 1972 by Kennikat Press
Library of Congress Catalog Card No: 79-159711
ISBN 0-8046-1672-8

Manufactured by Taylor Publishing Company   Dallas, Texas

ACKNOWLEDGMENTS

I wish to express my sincere thanks to the authors and publishers of the various works from which I have drawn, and in particular to the following :

Mr. Edward H. Tatum, *The United States and Europe, 1815–1823*, a study in the background of the Monroe Doctrine (University of California Press, Berkeley, California, 1939).

Professor Dexter Perkins, *The Monroe Doctrine, 1823–1826* (Cambridge, Mass., 1927) ; *The Monroe Doctrine, 1826–1867* (Johns Hopkins Press, Baltimore, 1933) ; *The Monroe Doctrine, 1867–1907* (Johns Hopkins Press, Baltimore, 1937).

Professor J. Fred Rippy, *The Rivalry between the United States and Great Britain over Latin America, 1808–1830* (Johns Hopkins Press, Baltimore, 1929).

Mr. Quincy Howe, *England Expects Every American to do His Duty* (Simon and Schuster, New York, 1937 ; Robert Hale, London).

Mr. Hamish Hamilton for permission to quote from the valuable series, *The United States in World Affairs* (Harper Brothers, New York).

Messrs. Dodd, Mead and Co., New York, for permission to quote from *Grover Cleveland*, by Allan Nevins.

Among other works consulted my profound acknowledgment is due to those of Professor Harold Temperley.

And finally I must express my deep appreciation to Mr. Marsden and Mr. Ellis and the members of the Reading Room staff of the British Museum, whose help has been invaluable in the preparation of this book.

CONTENTS

I.	The Monroe Doctrine	9
II.	The Treaty of Ghent and the Russian Question	25
III.	Rush's Dispatches	33
IV.	Canning's Position	44
V.	Adams's Position	51
VI.	Monroe's Position	64
VII.	The Message becomes Doctrine	69
VIII.	Mexican Adventure	78
IX.	The Panama Canal	86
X.	The First Venezuela Crisis, 1895	91
XI.	The Second Venezuela Crisis	101
XII.	Yankee Imperialism	112
XIII.	What the Lawyers Think	122
XIV.	A Latin-American Viewpoint	130
XV.	The Doctrine is no Menace	134
XVI.	The Case for Isolation	138
XVII.	Then and Now	147
XVIII.	After Munich	154
	Appendix	161
	Index	173

THE MONROE DOCTRINE AND WORLD PEACE

CHAPTER I

THE MONROE DOCTRINE

I

THE Monroe Doctrine was the direct result of a crisis in world politics in 1823. It was a statement of foreign policy designed by President Monroe and his Cabinet to meet the crises which threatened the country during the autumn of that year. Considering the comparative weakness of the United States at that time it is a matter of legitimate pride that the men who directed the nation's foreign policy had both the courage and the vision to act as they did.[1]

[1] There is a queer tradition which lurks in some American minds that a European, particularly an English diplomat, holds a mysterious advantage over the rough and ready American. Nothing could be more mistaken in fact. A glance at the writings of Benjamin Franklin during the Treaty negotiations with Britain in 1783 or the diaries of John Quincy Adams during the months previous to Monroe's message, will dispel any such illusions. Mr. Quincy Howe's famous book, *England Expects Every American to do His Duty*, is largely based on this peculiar assumption, and its wide circulation only goes to indicate how deeply the fallacy has taken root, and how difficult it must be to remove the

THE MONROE DOCTRINE AND WORLD PEACE

It is the purpose of this book to examine the crises of 1823 and the formation of the famous doctrine as well as to consider how this fundamental principle of American foreign policy might be presumed to operate in a present-day crisis. In 1823 the doctrine created a new Balance of Power, and effectively prevented the Western Hemisphere from becoming another European battleground.

In 1939 America again holds the Balance of Power in Mr. Roosevelt's *Narrowing World*. By discriminating in the supply of arms and munitions, by the maintenance of a powerful navy, she can become a decisive factor in international calculations.

In 1823 " The United States found itself in the very difficult position of a relatively weak nation attempting to maintain the *status quo* in the collapsing colonial empire of another weak Power then engaged in war." [1] The President James Monroe and his Foreign Secretary Adams met the difficulty by the formation of an independent foreign policy. It was a comprehensive statement of America's position in world politics, and although " it did not produce all the effects which ardent but uncritical writers have claimed for it, it did accomplish more than recent critics

---

suspicion that " every British proposal is designed to induce the United States to underwrite British interests " (Lord Lothian, *Observer*, February 26, 1939). On the other hand, British scepticism at the altitudinous moralities that drift across the Atlantic during every crisis is also based on a suspicion that the Yankees will talk from a safe distance—but that is about all. These difficulties which revolve about the question of isolation will be examined in a later chapter.

[1] Tatum, *The United States and Europe, 1815–1823*, p. 254.

THE MONROE DOCTRINE

admit. It was a truly national policy which could serve the United States as a guide and a defense."[1]

To a great many Americans the foreign policy of the United States is based, and should be based, upon two great principles: to uphold the Monroe Doctrine and to avoid foreign entanglements. In practice the ordinary citizen interprets these principles in simple terms; to him they mean briefly that Europe must keep out of the affairs of the New World, and that the United States must keep out of the affairs of Europe. " The general lay conception of neutrality seems to conform to these broad conceptions of foreign policy: it means little more than keeping out of war. These prevailing concepts, however, do not *per se* spell isolation; if this co-operation does not lead to 'involvement' there arises the practical question: How far does the United States feel that it can go in joint action with other Powers without danger of becoming involved? What contribution might it naturally be expected to make to the advancement of collective security? "[2]

Collective security has already given way to a new Balance of Power, but the same question is constantly being asked.

" No more foolish or mischievous mistake could be made than to deduce that America is drawn into the European issue for the sake of Britain and France. Nothing of the kind. Her own interests are at stake in the threat to what

[1] *Op. cit.*, pp. 273–74. [2] *U.S. in World Affairs, 1934–35*, p. 257.

THE MONROE DOCTRINE AND WORLD PEACE

Mr. Roosevelt calls 'this narrowing world.' It is a threat to the very sinews of civilized life, to the three essential conditions of political and human welfare such as are 'indispensable to Americans, now as always,' religion, democracy, and international good faith."[1]

A few Great Powers control at present the destinies of mankind. The history of the future is the history of the relations, friendly or otherwise, between them; the diplomacy of the future is the grouping and regrouping of these Powers with or against each other. "When the ruling Powers are so few how can it be supposed that the United States will be willing to stand aloof from the European controversies which involve the destinies of the world, or that it could stand aloof if it so desired? For good or evil, the United States has taken upon itself a share in the world's affairs, and cannot abdicate its responsibilities. There is no such thing for us as a quiet home-dwelling under our vine and fig tree: there is for us no Chinese Wall against trade or intercourse or political influence."[2]

This, it is surprising to learn, was written by a political essayist in 1902, in an article on the Monroe Doctrine.

In February 1939 the German newspapers carried headlines reading, "America Betrays Monroe Doctrine," and the London *Daily Telegraph* on 2nd February reported that Mr. Johnson, the American Assistant-Secretary for War

[1] *Observer*, January 8, 1939.
[2] A. B. Hart, *American Historical Society*, Vol. VII., p. 77.

THE MONROE DOCTRINE

spoke of " a possible defensive war against aggressors seeking world domination."

He declared that America must be strongly armed for the enforcement of the Monroe Doctrine.

What is this Monroe Doctrine that has such amazing vitality that it has become, not merely the interesting historical policy of a dead administration, but once again a formidable issue in the present world of conflict and crises?

2

In his message to Congress on December 2, 1823, President Monroe made the following statements:

> The occasion has been judged proper for asserting as a principle in which the rights and interests of the United States are involved, that the American continents, by the free and independent conditions which they have assumed and maintain are henceforth not to be considered as subjects for future colonization by any European Powers.
>
> In the wars of the European Powers in matters relating to themselves we have never taken any part, nor does it comport with our policy so to do. It is only when our rights are invaded or seriously menaced that we resent injuries or make preparations for our defense. With the movements in this hemi-

sphere we are of necessity more immediately connected, and by causes which must be obvious to all enlightened and impartial observors. The political system of the Allied Powers is essentially different in this respect from that of America. . . . We owe it therefore to candour and to the amicable relations existing between the United States and those Powers, to declare that we should consider any attempt on their part to extend their system to any portion of this hemisphere as dangerous to our peace and safety. With the existing colonies or dependencies of any European Power we have not interfered, and shall not interfere. But with the governments who have declared their independence and maintained it, and whose independence we have on great consideration and on just principles acknowledged we could not view any interposition for the purpose of oppressing them, or controlling in any other manner their destiny by any European Power in any other light than as the manifestation of an unfriendly disposition toward the United States.

In the war between those new governments and Spain we declared our neutrality at the time of their recognition, and to this we have adhered and shall continue to adhere, provided no change shall occur which, in the judgment of the competent authorities of this government, shall make a corresponding change on the part of the United States indispensable to their security. It is impossible that the Allied

THE MONROE DOCTRINE

Powers should extend their political system to any portion of either continent without endangering our peace and happiness ; nor can any one believe that our southern brethren, if left to themselves, would adopt it of their own accord. It is equally impossible, therefore, that we should behold such interposition in any form with indifference. If we look to the comparative strength and resources of Spain and these new governments, and their distance from one another, it must be obvious that she can never subdue them. It is still the true policy of the United States to leave the parties to themselves, in the hope that other Powers will pursue the same course.

There are, in these statements, four principles which form what has come to be known as the Monroe Doctrine.

The first is the non-colonization principle. " The American continents . . . are henceforth not to be considered as subjects for future colonization by any European Powers."

This was a general warning to Europe, and a particular warning to England. As we shall see the Russian claim to influence on the north-western coast south of parallel 55 was about to be withdrawn, and Russia was prepared to continue on friendly terms with the United States in spite of a diametrically opposed political ideology. The only Power with pretensions on the North American continent which could develop into a serious threat to the United States in 1823

THE MONROE DOCTRINE AND WORLD PEACE

was England. The Oregon question was unsettled, and the possible acquisition of Cuba by England was a constant source of anxiety to Monroe and his Cabinet. These two questions will be examined in their places. It is sufficient here to record Canning's reaction to this part of the message.

"How," he said to Richard Rush the American minister, "could America be closed to future British colonization, when American geographical limits were actually unknown? If we were to be repelled from the shores of America it would not matter to us whether that repulsion was effected by the ukase of Russia [1] excluding us from the sea, or by the new doctrine of the President excluding us from the land. But we cannot yield obedience to either." [2]

Canning therefore rejected and opposed the first great principle of the Doctrine, and it was not until seventy-five years had passed that British statesmen "finally commenced to disavow hostility toward the manifesto and ended by accepting it." [3]

It is necessary to stress this point at the beginning of this discussion, since there is a widespread fallacy that somehow or other the Monroe Doctrine was Canning's idea, and the benevolent presence of the British Navy made it possible to be announced.[4]

---

[1] September 7, 1821.
[2] *Cambridge History of British Foreign Policy*, Vol. II., p. 73.
[3] Rippy, *Rivalry between U.S. and Great Britain over Latin America, 1808–1830*, p. 314.
[4] Quincy Howe, *England Expects Every American to do His Duty*, p. 8.

THE MONROE DOCTRINE

Lord Lothian falls into this familiar mistake when he writes :

" So long as the British Navy was paramount on the sea, and the policy of the British Government was support of the Monroe Doctrine originally proposed by Canning, the British Navy acted in effect as the front line of defence for the United States and the whole Western Hemisphere."

This is at best a dangerous half-truth. It is true that no British minister would have seen a restoration of Spanish rule in South America with the direct or indirect interference by France (Canning in the House of Commons, Feb. 4, 1824), or any member of the Holy Alliance, and to this extent Adams and Monroe fully realized that the British Navy lay between Europe and the Western Hemisphere. On the other hand, Canning refused to move in concert with the United States upon the basis of the acknowledged independence of the South American States, and it became evident to Adams that England, not the Holy Alliance nor the Russian menace, was the chief danger to be met. But England's ambiguous position between the Holy Alliance and the United States was favourable to Adams, who took full advantage of it. " My reliance," he wrote, " upon the co-operation of Great Britain rested not upon her principles, but her interest—this I thought was clear."

England, therefore, was the key Power in the formation of the American Doctrine, and to counteract any moves that she might make in the Western Hemisphere was the purpose of the first principle of the message.

But another source of power and persuasion contributed, in the aggregate, a more important part to the background of the Doctrine than the British Navy. Americans had taken the measure of British ships in the late war, and, leaving mere numbers aside, had, ship for ship, beaten them in single combat more often than not. But American sensitiveness to criticism did not show the same intrepidness to the onslaughts of British ink, and the thin-skinned Americans found the sarcasm and condescension of the British Press more formidable than the broadsides of the British Navy. The sneering tone of superiority adopted after the Treaty of Ghent irritated a young nation, and English inventiveness added to the almost exhausted vocabulary of vituperation, an indecency and violence which has to be re-read to be believed.

The immediate result was an increased spirit of nationalism in America. English hatred was used as an argument for national defence and isolation, and the general feeling was expressed by an American scholar who loved England. "If," he wrote, "we can be connected with Great Britain on terms of mutual goodwill and mutual respect I shall hail the connection with the most sincere pleasure: but if the people of that country are to regard us with malignity and contempt, and to treat us with abuse and slander, the sooner and the farther we are separated the better"

THE MONROE DOCTRINE

There were many less restrained commentators than the Reverend Timothy Dwight,[1] President of Yale College, and the ingrained feeling of hostility which was created between 1815–23 has taken more than a century to subside. There is neither place nor space in this book for a full discussion of Anglo-American relations, fascinating though it would be in human character and conflict. But one perceives in looking at the background of Monroe's message that England had a considerable hand in its formation—though not exactly the hand of friendship.[2]

The second principle of the message was a maintenance of the *status quo*. "With the existing colonies or dependencies of any European Power we have not interfered and shall not interfere."

There is little comment to be made on this part of the Doctrine. The tacit allusion to Cuba was simply to the effect that any change in sovereignty would be to change the attitude of non-interference.

The third principle is the one which has done the most to make the Monroe Doctrine a living issue in world affairs at various times of crisis. The declaration of a political system different from that of Europe was on the face of it an answer to the manifesto of absolutism which the Tsar Alexander had recently announced to the world, but the qualification of this statement was a warn-

---

[1] Dwight, *Remarks*, Vol. VIII., etc.
[2] The general references are to be found in *The National Intelligencer*, *Niles Weekly Register*, *The Quarterly Review*, *The Edinburgh Review*, *The Pamphleteer*, *The North-American Review*, Irving's *Sketch Book*, Dwight's *Remarks*, etc.

ing to all European Powers. "We should consider any attempt on their part to extend their system to any portion of this hemisphere as dangerous to our peace and safety."

The fourth principle was the statement of non-interference of the United States in European affairs.

From the first glance at these four principles it is evident that the message was neither in the nature of a treaty nor the assertion of a point of international law: it was a manifesto of foreign policy, a statement that under certain circumstances the United States would act in certain ways.

In order to understand the conditions which led to the formation of the Doctrine a brief survey of world affairs during the preceding eight years is necessary.

3

In 1815 Russia, under the personal guidance of Tsar Alexander I., held a predominant position among the Continental Powers. The Tsar directed his own foreign policy, and the strength of his military establishments made him feared and respected by Metternich and Talleyrand. Austria and France were exhausted; Russia, with an army of a million men, was "a dangerous ally." Yet there is another aspect of Alexander I. which made him equally prominent in a reactionary world. He was the idol of the liberals, who looked to him to be "the arbiter of peace for the civilized world, the protector of the weak and oppressed, the guardian of international justice." They hoped that his reign would begin a new era in international politics; politics henceforth based on the general good and on the rights of each and all." [1]

Thus the opening of the Congress of Vienna had found two great currents of political opinion struggling against each other. The enthusiastic idealistic liberalism of Alexander I. backed by the youth of the world and a few veterans like Lafayette who never grew old, and the reactionary monarchs and statesmen whose one thought was to stop up all loopholes of liberalism, revolution, or reform. The success of the reactionary party spread despair among the liberals, which economic and financial chaos only tended to aggravate.

England's position demands special consideration. After twenty-two years of war the victory had left her apparently as entangled in European politics as any of the other Powers. Yet actually she held a different position from any of her allies or enemies. She was able to finance foreign governments through her great private banking firms at the same time as she was turning the enormous producing power that the industrial revolution was giving her into peaceful channels. She wanted to control the Balance of Power in a reorganized Europe, but at the same time she insisted on reserving a large degree of isolation for herself. A large and intelligent part of public

[1] Prince Czartoryski, *Memoirs*, quoted Tatum, *op. cit.*, p. 6.

THE MONROE DOCTRINE AND WORLD PEACE

opinion in the country was in avowed sympathy with liberal thought, and detested the sight of a Europe that was more fiercely reactionary than before the Revolution. Yet the government was not in the least interested in revolutionary or even liberal principles, and tended to favour the reactionary governments which had emerged from the Congress of Vienna. Above these conflicting tendencies the fact remained that England had emerged from the long struggle as the undisputed master of the seven seas, with sufficient power to block any move of any combination of powers not strictly limited to Continental action. " Sea power alone made England the beginning, the middle, and the end of all considerations of world policy, and it is impossible to over-emphasize this fact." [1]

This, then, being England's position in the world it is necessary to examine her relations with the United States at this period, since the effect of these relations was a determining factor in the formation of American foreign policy.

In 1815 Anglo-American relations were based on a " tradition of inveterate hostility, deep-seated hatred, and steady conflict. No man alive could remember a single hour when it could be truthfully said that England was friendly to the United States. From 1763–83 England was the oppressor of struggling colonies ; and from 1753–1815 she had been a high-handed tyrant over neutral commerce. . . . England had always been the enemy of the United

[1] Tatum, *op. cit.*, p. 16.

THE MONROE DOCTRINE

States, she always would be a determined foe. It was only a matter of time and circumstances until the two would have to fight again. Never would there be permanent peace until America had crushed England so completely that war would be impossible."[1]

Castlereagh's instructions to Stratford Canning on his appointment to Washington show how seriously the British Cabinet regarded the state of Anglo-American relations. After counselling him to conduct his business as much as possible by conversation because the government was given to contentious discussion, he wrote, "the American people are more easily excited against us and more disposed to strengthen the hands of their Ministers against this than against any other State."

Any examination of the Press of both countries during this period will show that this estimate is not exaggerated, and it is remarkably interesting to notice that three factors which to-day are constantly referred to, and in fact are reasons for close co-operation between the two countries, were for more than a quarter of a century among the principal reasons for violent antagonism : sea power, territorial possessions on the same continent ; a common language and heritage. Not only has the strategic position of both countries completely changed in a century, their relative strength and influence upon world affairs has also altered. It is no longer possible to draw a clear line of difference between European and

[1] Tatum, *op. cit.*, p. 33.

American questions. This aspect of the Doctrine must be reserved for its place, but there is no reason to obscure the historical background simply because the later and present relations between the two countries are fortunately increasingly harmonious.

Chapter II

THE TREATY OF GHENT AND THE RUSSIAN QUESTION

In 1815 the hatred between England and America was far greater than between America and any other nation. It was deeply rooted in half a century of unmitigated hostilities. It had recently been aggravated by a second war and a peace which was considered in America as making friendship possible but improbable, and in England as being " one of the most unfortunate acts of diplomacy in which Great Britain ever engaged." [1]

The end of the war only meant the beginning of a new commercial rivalry which in turn would lead to a new war. *Niles Weekly Register* (March 2, 1816) declared that, " If there be such things as a ' natural enmity ' between nations, Great Britain must be such an enemy of this Republic." This was not an isolated opinion, nor was it limited to American papers or American spokesmen. English papers commented freely and bitterly on America. Washington Irving refused an offer from the great John Murray to write for the *Quarterly Review*, giving as his reason that " the

[1] *Colonial Policy of Great Britain*, p. 181.

Quarterly has always been so hostile to my country."[1] It appeared to be as instinctive as the Englishman's dislike of the French, and based upon the same tradition of war and rivalry. Certainly it is an important consideration in estimating the causes of the famous Doctrine. Moreover, England's tremendous naval power, spread all over the world, appeared to Americans as a direct menace to their trade and commerce. England was the predominant Power in the world. Her wealth, her navy, and her possessions were more formidable in relation to the rest of the world than ever they would be again. She was the unchallenged centre of European commerce and finance. The continental countries were tied to her banks at the same time that they were struggling frantically to free themselves from her commercial supremacy.

Thus England's world position was vastly more important than Russia's, and it must be remembered that one of the possible combinations that Russia feared most was an alliance of Anglo-American policy. What hold Russia had on the North-West coast could not possibly be of any use to her if both naval powers were ranged against her. But before examining how Adams and Monroe managed to exclude Russia it is necessary to explain how she got there in the first place.

The Russian interest in the North-West coast of America can be briefly summarized. In 1727 the famous explorer, Vitus Behring, discovered the Straits which now bear his name. Fourteen years

[1] Mowat, *Americans in England*, p. 108.

later he sailed to the Alaskan coast,[1] and soon after his discoveries he was followed by fur traders who established posts on the adjacent islands. On July 8, 1799, the Tsar issued a ukase (an edict) creating a monopoly for the Russian-American Fur Company to trade as far south as latitude 55° and granting the Company the right to establish settlements on any unoccupied territory.[2] For the next twelve years little was heard in the political world of Russian penetration in the North-West. Occasional stories of New England captains trading along the coast, occasional complaints of the Russian Ambassador in Washington about this interference were not taken very seriously. England, rather than America, viewed the Russian Eastern expansion with alarm, and the Tsar on his side endeavoured to draw America into an alliance which would offset England's sea-power. Adams himself had been American minister to St. Petersburg; he had the incalculable advantage of knowing Alexander at a time when personalities in politics counted as definitely as they do to-day. He had then heard the expressed opinion of Russian diplomats that it was sound Russian policy to be friendly with the United States in order to offset English maritime pretensions, and he himself was prepared to meet such friendship if (1) American expansion on the continent was not menaced, (2) America was not drawn into a European alliance. Thus Russia would have liked to have had America as an ally in the Holy

[1] Latitude 58°.   [2] Perkins, *The Monroe Doctrine, 1823-1826*, p. 4.

Alliance, because American ships would be a valuable asset in the event of war with England. England was withdrawing from the European field and by 1820 was reviewing her position in the West, which must necessarily affect American interests.

For England, by the convention of 1818, held joint ownership with the United States of undefined territory north of latitude 42°. However, Adams refused to be drawn by the Russian advances. In his dispatch to his minister at St. Petersburg, on July 5, 1820, he was perfectly courteous to the Tsar, but he wrote that " the European and American political systems should be kept as separate and distinct from each other as possible." [1]

This was not a new idea in Adams's mind occasioned by the Tsar's proposals. In November of the previous year he had written in his diary that " the world must be familiarized with the idea of considering our proper dominion to be the continent of North America. From the time when we became an independent people it was as much a law of Nature that this should become our pretension as that the Mississippi should run into the sea." Nor did this expansionist idea originate with Adams. Both Franklin and Jefferson refer to it again and again in their writings, and it can be said without exaggeration to be one of the national ideas growing out of the Revolution and common to the thinking people of the country. Since this idea developed into

[1] Adams, *Memoirs*, Vol. VII., p. 50.

one of the basic statements of the Monroe Doctrine, to be known as the non-colonization principle, it is both interesting and necessary to trace its development and discover the cause for the great emphasis which Adams laid upon it. For without doubt this phase of the famous Doctrine was largely due to Adams's initiative and courage. The question was brought into prominence by the Tsar's ukase of 1821, but, in the various discussions and conversations which took place until the announcement of Monroe's message two years later, it is apparent that it was England and not Russia from whom Adams feared the greatest harm. England held the central position in world politics; England alone could do more damage to American expansion, American trade, and America's growing commercial and maritime interests than any combination of Powers. Moreover, France and Russia had every reason to make advances to America in order to restore the European Balance of Power in their favour; and an examination of American public opinion, which played an important part in shaping her foreign policy, will show that whereas jealousy and fear of England was widespread—and reciprocated—the feeling between the United States and Russia never reached a really dangerous crisis.

There were, it is true, a number of questions over which Russia and the United States might have clashed in a serious manner. But in every case Russia modified or changed her policy when faced with a definite declaration by Adams.

Thus Russia disapproved of the recognition of South America by the United States, but when it became evident that recognition would be accorded, Russia took pains to let the United States know that she had no hostile intentions against either continent. And Middleton, the American minister at St. Petersburg, reported that the policy of the United States had " in no degree impaired our good standing with the Emperor."

A more serious source of trouble lay in the dispute over Russian claims on the northwestern coast. Although the Russians had been there for some years, it was the Tsar's ukase of 1821 that brought the question into prominence. This extravagant document declared that Russia claimed absolute rights over territory as far south as latitude 51°, or four degrees south of the point claimed in the ukase of 1799. Furthermore, no foreign ships were to be allowed within 100 miles of the coast, and a Russian man-of-war was sent to enforce the decree.

The Russian ukase appeared preposterous on paper, but in practice it turned out to be of little importance. When Middleton read a note of protest from Adams to the Russian Foreign Secretary (July 4, 1822) he was advised not to present it to the Tsar, since "The Emperor has already had the good sense to see that this matter has been pressed too far. We are not disposed to follow it up." [1]

[1] *Alaskan Boundary Tribunal*, Vol. II., p. 43. Quoted by Perkins, *The Monroe Doctrine, 1823–1826*, p. 29.

TREATY OF GHENT AND RUSSIAN QUESTION

Nevertheless the Russian question was unsolved, and continued to form one of the complex group of circumstances which affected international relations until the autumn of 1823.

When Baron de Tuyll, the Russian Ambassador, called at the State Department on 17th July to inquire what instructions Adams was proposing to send to Middleton at St. Petersburg, he was told that " we should contest the right of Russia to any territorial establishment in this continent ; and that we should assume distinctly the principle that the American continents are no longer subjects for any new European colonial establishments."[1] Thus, four months before Monroe's speech, his Secretary of State had declared one of the basic principles of the Doctrine. It is true that the actual instructions to Middleton were not put in such strong language. Adams's phrasing did after all constitute a threat, but Russia was disposed to yield to it or ignore its implications rather than risk hostilities in the Pacific.

On 15th November Baron de Tuyll sent Adams some extracts from a dispatch which he had received from his Court, containing the Emperor's views on the affairs of Spain and a general statement of the principles of absolutism. This remarkable document gave Adams the opportunity he wanted. Here was the Holy Alliance proclaiming the virtues and glories of despotism. " If the Emperor set up to be the mouthpiece of Divine Providence it would be well to intimate

[1] Adams, *Memoirs*, Vol. VI., p. 163.

that this country did not recognize the language spoken, and had a destiny of its own, also under the guidance of Divine Providence. If Alexander could exploit his political principles, those of a brutal repressive policy, the United States could show that another system of government remote and separate from European traditions and administration could give rise to a new and more active political principle—the consent of the governed, between which and the Emperor there could not exist even a sentimental sympathy. . . .

It was no longer Canning who was to be answered, it was Europe." [1]

" My purpose," wrote Adams, " would be in a moderate and conciliatory manner, but with a firm and determined spirit, to declare or dissent from the principles avowed in those communications ; to assert those upon which our Government is founded, and while disclaiming all intention of attempting to propagate them by force, and all interference with the political affairs of Europe, to declare our expectation and hope that the European Powers will equally abstain from the attempt to spread their principles in the American hemisphere, or to subjugate by force any part of these continents to their will." [2]

But before considering Adams's masterful reply we must turn to Europe and consider Canning's position and his proposals to Richard Rush, the American Minister.

[1] Ford, *American Historical Review*, Vol. VIII., p. 32.
[2] Adams, *Memoirs*, Vol. VI., p. 194.

CHAPTER III

RUSH'S DISPATCHES

DURING 1822 the Congress of Verona had determined to restore Ferdinand to the Spanish throne by force of arms, and had given that congenial task to France. The members of the Congress, moreover, had given each other mutual pledges " to use all their efforts to put an end to representative government in whatever country it may exist in Europe." It did not need a great imaginative effort to push this idea of absolutism a step further. After Spain, then Spain's colonies —and after the colonies what would prevent the holy disciples of legitimacy from attacking the United States—" the one great example of a successful democratic revolution."

Between the Holy Alliance and any such ambitious plan stood the barrier of Great Britain. England opposed the pretensions of the Alliance, yet without openly breaking with it. She held aloof, formally protested, and yet kept her policy of neutrality in close touch with her commercial interests. She professed some fear of France's intentions; she regarded Cuba, still a loyal Spanish colony, with envious eyes; and even

THE MONROE DOCTRINE AND WORLD PEACE

during the discussions at the Congress of Verona in the autumn of 1822 Canning had told the Cabinet that "no questions relating to continental Europe can be more immediately and vitally important to Great Britain than those which relate to America."[1]

After the cession of Florida to the United States by the Treaty of February 22, 1819, there had been an outburst of anger in the British Press. "American rapacity" was attacked in bitter language, and a demand was put forward that England should bring about the transfer of Cuba to herself in order to counteract the growing rivalry of the United States. This was alarming to Americans, who realized that Cuba was the key to the Caribbean, and that with England entrenched there, the ancient enemy would lie as a perpetual menace across the trade routes. There were disturbing rumours in the American Press that England was using her influence with Spain to prevent the ratification of the Florida treaty at the same time that she was intriguing to gain a foothold in Cuba. Castlereagh, it is true, denied the truth of these persistent rumours, in answer to Rush's inquiries, but the fact remained that American suspicions were not allayed.[2] There was still the possibility that England might acquire it from Spain, and both London and Washington continued to watch the island with suspicious eyes, each fearing the other would occupy it first.

[1] Canning, Cabinet Memorandum, Nov. 1822.
[2] Tatum, *The United States and Europe, 1815–1823*, p. 162.

RUSH'S DISPATCHES

Both nations had squadrons cruising in Caribbean waters, ostensibly to put an end to the depredations of pirates. How great the importance of Cuba was in Canning's mind is evident in this same memorandum to the Cabinet. " It may be questioned," he wrote, " whether any blow that could be struck by any foreign power in any part of the world would have a more sensible effect on the interests of this country (than an American occupation of Cuba) and on the reputation of its Government." In Washington the Cabinet meetings during March (1823) were almost entirely concerned with the Cuban question, and Adams wrote tersely on the 15th—
" Cuba = Calhoun for war with England if she means to take Cuba; Thompson for urging the Cubans to declare themselves independent, *if* they can maintain their independence." [1]

Jefferson also was more perturbed over Cuba than any other aspect of the international crises. " Cuba alone," he wrote to Monroe, " seems at present to hold up a speck of war to us. Its possession by Great Britain would indeed be a great calamity to us. Could we induce her to join us in guaranteeing its independence against all the world, except Spain, it would be nearly as valuable as if it were our own. But should she take it, I would not immediately go to war for it ; because the first war on other accounts will give it to us, or the island will give itself to us when able to do so."

At the State Department Adams was equally

[1] Adams, *Memoirs*, Vol. VI.

THE MONROE DOCTRINE AND WORLD PEACE

alert. In his instructions to Hugh Nelson, the American minister in Spain,[1] he made his position clear.

"You will not conceal from the Spanish Government," he wrote, " the repugnance of the United States to the transfer of the Island of Cuba by Spain to any other power. The deep interest which would to them be involved in the event gives them the right of objecting against it: and as the People of the Island itself are known to be averse to it, the right of Spain itself to make the cession, at least on the principles on which the present Spanish constitution is founded, is more than questionable." It is interesting to see Adams setting up the principle of self-determination as a natural American heritage at a time when reaction against all forms of liberal or representative doctrine was being actively supported by the European monarchs.

On 16th August Canning unexpectedly sounded Rush concerning a joint policy toward the former Spanish colonies. "Not," as he added, "that any concert in action under it could become necessary between the two countries, but that the simple fact of our being known to hold the same sentiment would he had no doubt by its moral effect, put down the intention on the part of France, admitting that she had ever entertained it." This belief was founded, he said, "upon the large share of the maritime power of the world which Great Britain and the United States share between them and the consequent influence

[1] April 28, 1823.

which the knowledge that they hold a common opinion upon a question on which such large maritime interests present and future hung, could not fail to produce upon the rest of the world." [1]

Rush was at first impressed by this approach, and four days later he forwarded to Adams a private and confidential note from Canning embodying under five headings his ideas for a joint policy. They were as follows :

(1) We conceive the recovery of the Colonies by Spain to be hopeless.
(2) We conceive the question of the recognition of them as Independent States to be one of time and circumstance.
(3) We are, however, by no means disposed to throw any impediment in the way of an arrangement between them and the mother country by amicable negotiations.
(4) We aim not at the possession of any portion of them for ourselves.
(5) We could not see any portion of them transferred to any other Power with indifference.

" If these opinions and feelings are, as I firmly believe them to be, common to your Government with ours, why should we hesitate mutually to confide them to each other and to declare them in the face of the world ? " [2]

---
[1] Rush, *Court of London*, p. 401.
[2] *Ibid.*, pp. 401-402.

This important communication was immediately forwarded to Adams, whose replies to these points will appear in due course. Here it is only necessary to remark on point No. 2. The United States had already recognized the new States, and when a few days later Canning showed " an extraordinary change of tone," and made it evident that he was not prepared to agree to immediate recognition, Rush's suspicions were aroused.

" I am bound to own," he wrote to Monroe, " that I shall not be able to avoid, at bottom, some distrust of the motive of all such advances to me, whether directly or indirectly, by this Government at this particular juncture of the world." [1]

It is clear that Canning was perfectly well aware that his own intransigence was holding up any joint action. He wrote Bagot,[2] " that Rush had told him in the previous August that he would say, swear, sign, anything *sub spiritu* if the British Government would place itself in the same line as the United States by acknowledging the South American States." However, Canning certainly could not have got the consent of either Cabinet or King in 1823, and he himself seems to have doubted of its wisdom at the moment.[3]

A few of Rush's letters will complete the account of these negotiations, in which it became

[1] *American Historical Review*, Vol. VII., p. 687.
[2] January 9, 1824.
[3] Temperley, *Foreign Policy of Canning*, p. 113.

evident that the American Government quickly realized the impossibility of acting with England.

Rush to Monroe, September 15, 1823

The estimate which I have formed of the genius of this Government, as well as of the characters of the men who direct, or who influence, all its operations, would lead me to fear that we are not yet likely to witness any very material changes in the part which Britain has acted in the world for the past fifty years, when the cause of freedom has been at stake : the part which she acted in 1774 in America, which she has since acted in Europe, and is now acting in Ireland. I shall therefore find it hard to keep from my mind the suspicion that the approaches of her ministers to me at this portentous juncture for a concert of policy which they have not heretofore courted with the United States, are bottomed on their own calculations. I wish that I could sincerely see in them a true concern for the rights and liberties of mankind.[1]

Rush to Adams, October 2, 1823

He [Canning] had declared that this Government felt great embarrassments as regarded the immediate recognition of these new states,

[1] *Massachusetts Historical Society*, Vol. XV., p. 421.

embarrassments which had not been common to the United States, and asked whether I could not give my assent to his proposals on a promise by Great Britain of *future* acknowledgment. To this intimation I gave an immediate and unequivocal refusal. . . .

I cannot be unaware that in this whole transaction the British Cabinet are striving for their own ends : yet if these ends promise in this instance to be also auspicious to the safety and independence of Spanish America, I persuade myself that we cannot look upon them but with approbation. England it is true has given her countenance, and still does, to all the evils with which the Holy Alliance has afflicted Europe : but if she at length has determined to stay the career of their formidable and despotick ambition in to this hemisphere, the United States seem to owe it to all the policy and to all the principles of their system to hail the effects whatever may be the motives of her conduct.[1]

In his long letter to Adams of October 10, 1823, Rush did not hide the bitter disappointment he felt at Canning's change of front.

" I saw him [Canning] again," he wrote, " at the Foreign Office yesterday, and he said not one single word relative to South America, although the occasion was altogether favourable for resuming the topick, had he been disposed to resume it. . . .

[1] *Op. cit.*, p. 424.

"The termination of the discussion between us may be thought somewhat sudden, not to say abrupt considering how zealously as well as spontaneously it was started on his side. As I did not commence it, it is not my intention to revive it.[1]

"Whether any fresh explanations of France since the fall of Cadiz may have brought Mr. Canning to so full and sudden a pause with me, I do not know, and most likely never shall know if events so fall out that Great Britain no longer finds it necessary to seek the aid of the United States in furtherance of her scheme of counter action against France or Russia. That the British Cabinet and the governing portion of the British nation, will rejoice at heart in the downfall of the constitutional system in Spain, I have never had a doubt and have not now, so long as this catastrophe can be kept from crossing the path of British interests and British ambition. This nation in its collective, corporate capacity has no more sympathy with popular rights and freedom now than it had on the plains of Lexington in America : than it showed during the whole progress of the Revolution in Europe or at the close of its first great act, at Vienna in 1815 : than it exhibited lately in Naples in proclaiming a neutrality in all other events save that of the safety of the royal family there : or, still more recently when it stood aloof whilst France and the Holy Alliance avowed their intention of crushing the liberties of unoffending Spain, of

[1] *Op. cit.*, p. 425.

crushing them too upon pretexts so wholly unjustifiable and enormous that English Ministers, for very shame, were reduced to the dilemma of speculatively protesting against them, whilst they allowed them to go into full action." [1]

To say that Rush was perplexed is to put it mildly. He could do no more than reflect that his own conduct had been true to the principles of his Government, and that it now rested with his superiors to act upon the information contained in his dispatches.

As far as he was concerned there was nothing more to be done.

" The Spanish topic," he concluded in his letter to Monroe,[2] " has been dropped by Mr. Canning in a most extraordinary manner. Not another word has he said to me on it since the 26th of last month at the interview at Gloucester Lodge, which I have described in my despatches to the Department, and he has now gone out of town to spend the remainder of this and part of next month. I shall not renew the topick, and should he, which I do not expect, I shall decline going into it again, saying that I must now wait until I hear from my government."

However, the negotiations between Rush and Canning continued on the 24th November, when Canning informed the American minister that he had thought it necessary to come to some agreement with France over the South American question. Rush duly forwarded the information

[1] *Op. cit.*, p. 426.
[2] *Op. cit.*, p. 426.

to Adams on 27th November, but by the time it reached Washington the famous message had been delivered to Congress and the Doctrine was on its way to England. Canning was still showing " extraordinary solicitude for secrecy," which was in Rush's opinion due to " an unwillingness in this government to risk the cordiality of its standing with the Holy Alliance to any greater extent than can be avoided."

But the message completely altered the situation. " It was," wrote Rush, " the most decisive blow to all despotick interference with the new States. . . . It was looked for here with extraordinary interest at this juncture, and I have heard that the British packet which left New York the beginning of this month was instructed to wait for it and bring it over with all speed. . . . On its publicity in London which followed as soon afterwards as possible the credit of all the South American securities immediately rose, and the question of the final and complete safety of the new States from all European coercion is now considered at rest." [1]

[1] *Op. cit.*, p. 436.

CHAPTER IV

CANNING'S POSITION

APPARENTLY Canning had feared French designs on South America. " France meditates and has all along meditated a direct interference in Spanish America." [1] It was common knowledge that the French were prepared to support the planting of Bourbon Princes in Mexico and Peru. The President of the French Council, Villèle, had declared that the French expedition then fitting out in the harbours of France would be at the orders of the Spanish Government if it wished to send an Infant to any port of Spanish America. In order to clear up this position Canning attempted to come to an agreement with Polignac. But before doing so he had, as we have seen, approached Rush and attempted to get America to come to an " understanding." Rush had welcomed the suggestion and forwarded the proposals to Washington. But the point of difference—the recognition of the new States— had proved insuperable and the negotiations broke down. Baffled by Adams's independent

[1] To Wellington, September 24, 1823.

CANNING'S POSITION

stand,[1] Canning moved alone and successfully against the French, making it perfectly plain that England would oppose any French attack on South America. From the American point of view this was a welcome move as far as it went. But Canning went further than this. He was ready to admit that monarchic and aristocratic principles could be encouraged in Mexico, Peru, and Chili, and he was playing a waiting game to see whether or not the new nations would follow the American republican idea or the European monarchic idea. He did not object to some of the South American States being republics. It would give a better balance both to the continent and the world.[2] But Adams was now convinced that England as well as France and Russia should all be faced with a policy that would clearly define America's position in the western world. The moment had come to " make up an American policy and adhere inflexibly to that," and at the same time he would " prevent the United States from circulating as a satellite in the orbit of Great Britain." [3]

" The plain Yankee of the matter is, that the United States wish to monopolize to themselves the colonizing of that [the North-West coast] and every other part of the American Continent in a similar condition . . . and an attempt to give a

---

[1] Adams took a firm stand against French designs, " It is impossible," he wrote to his envoy in Paris, " that *any* American interest should be served by importing a petty Prince from Europe to make him a king in America." Adams feared political and commercial subservience to European interests.

[2] Temperley, *Foreign Policy of Canning*, p. 139.

[3] *Ibid.*, p. 123.

THE MONROE DOCTRINE AND WORLD PEACE

show of *right* to a mere arbitrary assumption partakes a little of the simplicity and integrity which are said to be elements of the Republicans character." [1]

The *Star* was essentially correct in its estimate, and its dislike of the Yankee of the matter was shared by Canning himself who immediately repudiated the non-colonization clause as inadmissible. Many people and some newspapers in England, however, professed to see the Doctrine as a mere carrying out of Canning's suggestions. " But to the United States the message made a different appeal. The United States seemed to stand forth and claim the place of leader among the American peoples, and to the ordinary citizen the ban upon adventure in the New World appeared to be directed at least as much against Great Britain and her supposed designs on Cuba as against the Continental Powers of whom much less was known." [2]

It is true that the Doctrine was a warning to Europe, but it was Europe as America conceived it, and that was the Europe which included Canning.

That Canning himself realized this is evident. He favoured monarchy in Mexico and Brazil precisely because it " would cure the evils of universal democracy and prevent the drawing of the line of demarcation which I most dread —America *versus* Europe.

" The United States, naturally enough, aim

[1] The *Star*, December 27, quoted by Temperley.
[2] *Cambridge History of British Foreign Policy*, Vol. II., p. 231.

CANNING'S POSITION

at this division and cherish the democracy which leads to it." [1]

But if Canning failed in North America he succeeded brilliantly in South America.

" In all that related to the matter of prestige England appears to have had some advantage from start to finish and it was perhaps natural that she should. Britain was the wealthiest country in the world, the mistress of the seas, the object of the admiration or of the envy and apprehension of every nation, with an experienced grasp of diplomats and consuls. The United States was young, small in population, comparatively poor, and somewhat careless in the training of its agents. Moreover the Yankees were greedily in pursuit of Spanish American territory, while Englishmen, with few minor exceptions, not only sought none, but made a futile effort to prevent the United States from acquiring any." [2]

The key to Canning's policy lay in his attempt to counteract the growing maritime and commercial importance of the United States. " There can be no doubt that to the end of his life Canning distrusted and disliked the United States and he was determined that she should not obtain control of her Southern neighbours." [3]

A number of points in his memoranda to the Cabinet make this clear.

" Sooner or later," he wrote in 1824, " we shall probably have to contend with the com-

[1] Temperley, *Foreign Policy of Canning*, p. 129.
[2] Rippy, *Rivalry between U.S. and Great Britain over Latin America, 1808–1830*, p. 309.
[3] Petrie, *Canning*, p. 189.

bined maritime power of France and the United States. The disposition of the new states is at present highly favourable to England. If we take advantage of that disposition we may establish through our influence with them a fair counterpoise to that combined maritime power. Let us not then throw the present golden opportunity away, which once lost may never be recovered."

In another memorandum he referred to his " apprehension of the ambition and ascendancy of the United States of America. It is obviously the policy of that Government to connect itself with all the Powers of America in a general Trans-Atlantic league, of which it would have the sole direction. I need not say how inconvenient such an ascendancy may be in time of peace, and how formidable in case of war.

" I believe we now have the opportunity (but it may not last long) of opposing a powerful barrier to the influence of the United States by an amicable connection with Mexico, which from its position must be either subservient to or jealous of the United States . . . but if we hesitate much longer . . . all the new states will be led to conclude that we reject their friendship upon principle as if a dangerous and revolutionary character, and will be driven to throw themselves under the protection of the United States as the only means of security."

And when finally Canning had been able to overcome the opposition to recognition he wrote triumphantly to Granville : " The deed is done,

CANNING'S POSITION

the nail is driven. Spanish America is free ! and if we do not mismanage our affairs sadly *she is English*."

This remark must be carefully qualified. The non-colonization clause and the independent tone of the message conflicted directly with British interests, and it is not an exaggeration to maintain that the message as Adams and Monroe conceived it was first and foremost a stand against Britain. Any claims to Cuba or the North-West were henceforth impossible without coming into conflict once again with the United States. The Doctrine was in a sense the diplomatic conclusion of the war of 1812–14.

Canning it is true was a great enough statesman to accept the fact and turn his attention to his commercial policy in South America. In this he was brilliantly successful, and was somewhat justified in writing that "the effect of this ultra-liberalism of our Yankee co-operation gives me just the balance that I wanted."

The implications quickly became evident. The English delegate to the Congress of Panama was instructed to support any South American claim to Cuba as England could not agree to the occupation of the island by the United States.[1] Canning's famous sentence, "I called the New World into existence to redress the balance of the old," was far from being true. The balance that Canning was trying to redress was the preponderance in the affairs of the American continents which President Monroe had an-

[1] Mowat, *Great Britain and the United States*, p. 95.

THE MONROE DOCTRINE AND WORLD PEACE

nounced would be the rôle of the United States.[1]

[1] A comparison of the two countries' trade with South America shows:

	Britain less than		United States less than
In 1808	£5,000,000	In 1808	£6,000,000
In 1822	£6,000,000	In 1822	£3,000,000
In 1825	£12,000,000	In 1825	£5,000,000
In 1830	£6,400,000	In 1830	£4,000,000

The investment side of the picture is even more in Britain's favour. America had little or no capital to invest abroad, and what little ventures there were are insignificant. Britain, however, had some £210,000,000 invested in Spanish America by 1830.

Chapter V

ADAMS'S POSITION

On November 25, 1823, Adams drafted his observations on the Tsar's pronouncement. " It was," wrote Adams, " drawn to correspond exactly with a paragraph of the President's message which he read me yesterday and which was entirely conformable to the system of policy which I have earnestly recommended for this emergency. It was also intended as a firm, spirited and yet conciliatory answer to all the communications lately received from the Russian Government, and at the same time an unequivocal answer to the proposals made by Canning to Mr. Rush. It was meant also to be eventually an exposition of the principles of this Government, and a brief development of its political system as henceforth to be maintained : essentially republican—maintaining its own independence, and respecting that of others ; essentially pacific —studiously avoiding all involvement in the combinations of European politics, cultivating peace and friendship with the most absolute monarchies, highly appreciating and anxiously desirous of retaining that of the Emperor Alexander, but declaring that, having recognized the independence of South American States we could not see with indifference any attempt by European Powers by forcible interposition either to restore the Spanish dominion on the American continent or to introduce monarchial principles into those countries or to transfer any portion of the ancient or present American possessions of Spain to any other European power."

After a three days' discussion in the Cabinet, Adams's observations on the communications recently received from the Minister of Russia were agreed to with the exception of two paragraphs, and the reply was read to Baron de Tuyll on 27th November. This statement of republican principles was received with the utmost friendliness by the Russian, who assured Adams that he was perfectly sure of the friendly disposition of the Emperor toward the United States. "The Imperial Government," he said, "distinguished clearly between a republic like that of the United States and rebellion founded on revolt against legitimate authority." The interview ended with the most urbane expressions of courtesy and mutual esteem. But Adams had said what he wanted to say, and the fact that he now knew that Russia would not act in any way that would bring on a crisis strengthened his position in no small degree. Three days later he took full advantage of this in his dispatch to Rush in London.

This was in brief a declaration of the famous Doctrine. Adams was perfectly aware that Canning was not thinking of a policy of Anglo-

ADAMS'S POSITION

American friendship when he approached Rush, but was trying to use America " as a pawn in the game he was playing against France and the Holy Alliance."

" If," wrote Adams, " the Holy Allies should subdue Spanish America, however they might at first set up the standard of Spain, the ultimate result of this undertaking would be to recolonize them, partitioned out among themselves. Russia might take California, Peru, Chili ; France Mexico—where we know she has been intriguing to get a monarchy under a Prince of the House of Bourbon, as well as at Buenos Ayres. And Great Britain as her last resort, if she could not resist the course of things, would at least take the Island of Cuba for her share of the scramble . . . the danger, therefore, was brought to our own doors and I thought we could not too soon take our stand to repel it."

There was, however, another possibility in the situation which equally perturbed Adams. Suppose the Holy Alliance should attack South America and be resisted by Britain alone. In Adams's opinion Britain would come out the victor in such a contest by her command of the sea. And South America would be entirely in her hands " and as the result make them her colonies instead of those of Spain. My opinion was therefore that we must act promptly and decisively." [1]

This then being Adams's state of mind, he had to face a number of problems of extreme gravity.

[1] Adams, *Memoirs*, Vol. VI., pp. 207–8.

THE MONROE DOCTRINE AND WORLD PEACE

The United States was a relatively weak nation and held little or no bargaining power against the greatest maritime nation in the world. Canning's friendly approach to Rush and his subsequent cooling off awakened a host of fears in America. The Press was full of alarm concerning the state of Europe. The Country was demanding that an answer be given to the Russian manifesto of absolutism and at the same time there should be a clear answer of the United States to Canning's proposals.

Between 11th September (1823) and 7th November there are unfortunately no entries in Adams's diary, so we can only surmise what effect Canning's advances produced on the Cabinet. Upon Monroe it is certain they produced an immediate and profound effect, for he turned at once to Jefferson and Madison, both of them former Presidents, for advice.

In his letter to Jefferson [1] he wrote that his own impression was, "that we ought to meet the proposal of the British Government and to make it known that we would view an interference on the part of the European Powers, and especially an attack on the Colonies by them, an attack on ourselves, presuming that if they succeeded with them they would extend it to us."

Both Jefferson and Madison replied with letters of advice. Jefferson's letter remains one of the classic statements of American foreign policy. Jefferson saw clearly that if America wanted to hold the Balance of Power and the

[1] October 17, 1823.

ADAMS'S POSITION

status quo on the two Continents she should not interfere in the broils of Europe. The interests of North and South America were separated from those of Europe.

" It would be advantageous," he wrote, " to meet Canning's proposals, not so much in order to block the Holy Alliance as to block any move that England might be tempted to make toward Cuba, as well as to prevent her from joining the Holy Alliance in any South American adventure. Great Britain is the nation which can do us the most harm of any one on all the earth. With her then, we should most sedulously cherish a cordial friendship ; and nothing would tend more to knit our affections than to be fighting once more side by side, in the same cause. Not that I would purchase even her amity at the price of taking part in her wars. But the war in which the present proposition might engage us, should that be its consequence, is not her war, but ours. . . . And if to facilitate this, we can effect a division in the body of the European powers, and draw over to our side its most powerful member, surely we should do it. . . . With Great Britain withdrawn from their scale and shifted into our two continents, all Europe combined would not undertake such a war. For how would they propose to get at either enemy without superior fleets ? "

There was, in Jefferson's opinion, one great disadvantage. If America agreed to Canning's proposals she would be unable to acquire Cuba. " Yet," wrote Jefferson, " as I am sensible that this can never be obtained even with her own consent, but by war ; and its independence which is our second interest, [and especially its independence of England] can be secured without it, I have no hesitation in abandoning my first wish to future chances and accepting its independence with grace and the friendship of England, rather than its association, at the expense of war and her enmity."

However, Rush's subsequent dispatches reporting Canning's change of tone brought the matter to a crisis, and both Adams and Monroe realized that it was absolutely necessary to form and declare an independent policy. Adams was particularly clear-headed about the situation, and throws a penetrating light upon the difference in character between himself and Monroe. "The President," he wrote, "is often afraid at this juncture of the skittishness of mere popular prejudices, and I am always disposed to brave them. I have much more confidence in the calm and deliberate judgment of the people than he has."

On 7th November the Cabinet considered Canning's "confidential" proposal to Rush and the correspondence between them relating to the projects of the Holy Alliance upon South America.

Monroe's attitude is noteworthy. Adams declares that the President was averse to any course which should have the appearance of taking a position subordinate to that of Great Britain.

ADAMS'S POSITION

But it was Adams who saw clearly the policy to pursue. The United States *had already* recognized the South American independence. Therefore Canning's proposals were neither useful nor proper. "The Russian situation," remarked Adams, "gave the United States the opportunity to take our stand against the Holy Alliance and at the same time to decline the overture of Great Britain. It would be more candid as well as more dignified to avow our principles explicitly to Russia and France than to come in as a cockboat in the wake of the British man-of-war." [1]

This idea was acquiesced in on all sides. Moreover, Adams realized clearly that the whole question of American foreign policy was rapidly coming to a crisis. The various instructions to the Ambassadors at London, Paris, and St. Petersburg must, he declared, "all be parts of a combined system of policy and adapted to each other."

From now on until the famous Doctrine was given to the world events moved quickly, and under the stress the characters of the men concerned stand out in greater relief. On 13th November Adams was occupied in "making a draft of minutes for the message of the President upon subjects under the direction of the Department of State."

"I find him," wrote Adams, "yet altogether unsettled in his own mind as to the answer to be given to Mr. Canning's proposals, and alarmed, far beyond anything I could have conceived

[1] Adams, *Memoirs*, Vol. VI., p. 178.

possible, with the fear that the Holy Alliance are about to restore immediately all South America to Spain.

"He will recover from this in a few days, but I never saw more indecision in him. We discussed the proposals of Canning, and I told him if he would decide either to accept or decline them I would draft a despatch conformable to either decision for his consideration."

"I thought," wrote Adams, "we should bring the whole answer to Mr. Canning's proposals to a test of right and wrong. Considering the South Americans as independent nations, they themselves, and no other nation had the *right* to dispose of their condition. *We* have no right to dispose of them, either alone or in conjunction with other nations. Neither have any other nations the right of disposing of them without their consent. This principle will give us a clue to answer all Mr. Canning's questions with candour and confidence, and I am to draft a despatch accordingly." [1]

Adams's reply to Canning's proposals was masterful. He was addressing not only England but all Europe. The Tsar had invoked Divine Providence, and put forward the Holy Alliance as the particular means by which he proposed that Divinity should act among nations—brute force, repression, and autocratic rule. It was time that another voice be heard in no uncertain terms.

The dispatch was addressed to Rush, but it

[1] Adams, *Memoirs*, Vol. VI., p. 186.

ADAMS'S POSITION

was meant for Russian and French ears quite as much as for Mr. Canning. After commending Rush for his behaviour, Adams took up Canning's points one by one.

1. *We conceive the recovery of the colonies by Spain to be hopeless.*

"In this we concur."

2. *We conceive the question of the recognition of them as independent to be one of time and circumstances.*

Adams's reply to this equivocal statement was to point out that the United States had already recognized their independence, and that it appeared to him to be a moral obligation on the part of Great Britain to recognize them if, as the first principle stated, she had conceived their recovery to be hopeless.

3. *We are, however, by no means disposed to throw any impediment in the way of an arrangement between them and the mother country by amicable negotiations.*

"Nor are we. . . . But," added Adams, "the arrangement must be upon a political and commercial footing equal to the most favoured nation." And here it is important to notice that Adams was as concerned with the commercial interests as Canning was, and, in general, Adams regarded commercial policy as equally important to the nation's interests as any political blocking of foreign territorial ambitions. Hitherto colonization had implied commercial monopoly, and, as Perkins rightly emphasizes, "Adams based this aspect of his foreign policy on a principle similar to the open-door principle and the liberalization of trade policies which Mr. Hull is contending

THE MONROE DOCTRINE AND WORLD PEACE

for with such earnestness." [1] The right to trade was, according to Adams, as important as the right to possess, since the right to possess had hitherto excluded the right to trade. Spain, for example, had excluded foreigners upon pain of death; and although English practice regarding her former colonies had not included the death penalty, Americans had suffered from and fought against the Navigation Laws for a generation.

" The whole system of modern colonization was an abuse of government, and it was time that it should come to an end," said Adams to the English Ambassador, Stratford Canning, in November, 1822.[2]

Points number 4 and number 5 concerning *no possession by ourselves, and no transference to another power* were fully agreed to. But Adams took occasion to express his own opinion about possible joint action, and it must be confessed that he carried off the honours of the situation in no uncertain manner. The two parts in brackets were not included in the draft finally sent, but they are included here because they help to illuminate the character of the great Secretary of State.

" We add," he wrote, " that we could not see with indifference any attempt [by one or more powers of Europe to dispose of the Freedom or Independence of those States without their consent or against their will]."

---

[1] Perkins, *op. cit.*, p. 17.
The modern problem created by colonies, and the recurrence of the monopoly, is most ably discussed in *The International Share-out*, Ward (Nelson and Sons), and will not be pursued here.
[2] Adams, *Memoirs*, Vol. VI., p. 104.

ADAMS'S POSITION

" [To this principle, in our view of this subject all the rest are subordinate. Without this, our concurrence with Great Britain upon all the rest would be useless.] It is upon this ground alone as we conceive that a firm and determined stand could now be jointly taken by Great Britain and the United States in behalf of the *Independence of nations*, and never in the history of mankind was there a period when a stand so taken and maintained would exhibit to present and future ages a more glorious example of power, animated by justice, and devoted to the ends of benevolence."[1]

In a private dispatch to Rush the following day Adams discussed Canning's position with great discernment. He pointed to Canning's avowed reasons to non-recognition as being so feeble that they played into America's hands. Canning might intimate that Great Britain was involved with other European nations whereas the United States had never interfered in the complications of European politics and, therefore, Great Britain would reserve judgment concerning South America. But Adams could remark that such independence of policy on the part of Britain was admissible with regard to Europe.

" But American Affairs whether of the Northern or of the Southern Continent *can* henceforth not be excluded from the interference of the United States." In other words, a situation which Canning may have hoped to lead and control as a European affair, with the United States as a concurring member in a new

[1] Ford, *Massachusetts Historical Society*, Vol. XV., p. 384.

Balance of Power, was being altered to an American affair controlled by Adams's bold and independent attitude. Naturally Canning's prevarication about recognition aroused suspicion. What had led the English Foreign Secretary to change from " the peculiar earnestness and solemnity of his first advances " to Rush to an apparent coolness and apparent indifference ?

" The object of Canning," wrote Adams,[1] " appears to have been to obtain some public pledge from the government of the United States ostensibly against the possible interference of the Holy Alliance between Spain and South America, but really or especially against the acquisition to the United States themselves of any part of the Spanish American possessions. . . . By joining with her therefore in her proposed declaration we give her a substantial and perhaps inconvenient pledge against ourselves, and really obtain nothing in return." [2]

Canning failed to draw America into even a partial alliance, as he was unable to meet Rush's primary condition of an immediate recognition of South American independence.[3] In fact, in the formation of the Doctrine Britain was not consulted at all, and she could only regard it as directly opposed to her own interests.[4]

" Viewed in the light of world politics and the realities of America's position, it (the Monroe Doctrine) appears in a different guise—it repre-

---

[1] Adams, *Memoirs*, Vol. VI., p. 177. [2] November 7, 1823.
[3] Ford, *American Historical Review*, Vol. VII., p. 691.
[4] Perkins, *op. cit.*, p. 32.

ADAMS'S POSITION

sents the outmanœuvring of a strong Power by a weak one. It made plain to England that war would probably result from further extensions of her influence in the New World. Either she must fight or renounce the idea of possessing Cuba and establishing new posts in the Oregon country. The Monroe Doctrine was no guarantee of protection to the United States, but it did make the policy of this country clear to all who chose to read. The dangers of foreign connections were avoided, the United States remained free, and England was caught in the mesh of her own tangled policy. The English Government was blocked not only by the threat contained in the Monroe Doctrine, but also by the fact that the declaration appealed to the widespread sentiments of the masses of the English people." [1]

[1] Tatum, *The United States and Europe, 1815–1823*, p. 274.

Chapter VI

MONROE'S POSITION

It is now necessary to examine Monroe's position. It has been customary of late to belittle his part in the crisis, and to represent him as a very timid man, unlikely to take so extreme a stand in the face of allied Europe.[1] He has in turn found his defenders, and a first-class controversy has been generated—a controversy which it is entirely useless to enter into in this discussion. Monroe was the chief member of the administration. Upon him fell the responsibility in the last analysis. He was, it must be remembered, as experienced a diplomat as Adams was. His nationalism and his republicanism were equally well tried, and his judgment was in the opinion of his own colleagues extraordinarily well balanced. "Above all the President recognized capacity and rose above sectional predilections in his appointment of John Adams as secretary of state. No choice for that great office has ever been a happier one, and the large discretion which Monroe left to Adams while yet maintaining a supervision over foreign affairs is highly creditable to him."[2]

[1] *Massachusetts Historical Society*, Vol. XV., p. 373.
[2] Perkins, *Dictionary American Bibliography*, Vol. VIII., p. 91.

MONROE'S POSITION

The two men worked together with remarkable harmony, and all through the caustic pages of Adams's diaries there is evidence of the great respect which he held for his chief, and Monroe, on his side, showed restraint and understanding in dealing with his forthright Secretary of State. There is no doubt at all that the initiative as well as the responsibility for the message belong to Monroe, but there is also no doubt that the so-called non-colonization principle was accepted by Monroe from Adams's report. Moreover, in November 1823 it appears that the nature of the crisis had taken more definite form with Adams than it had with Monroe.

Monroe's attitude is especially interesting at this point. It is clear that his mind had not grasped the situation with the vigorous certitude that Adams had already displayed. Even as late as 21st November (1823) he wrote in a note to Adams that he intended to bring up for Cabinet discussion " the important question whether any and if any, what notice shall be taken of Greece and also of the invasion of Spain by France." [1]

In Adams's mind, on the other hand, this question was already resolved. To intervene in Greece or to challenge the Holy Alliance in Europe was outside the question. It was dangerous policy, and it destroyed the strength which the Government would obtain by limiting the present crisis to a purely American policy. To be sure the policy affected the world Balance of Power, but it did not go crusading beyond the

[1] *Massachusetts Historical Society*, Vol. XV., p. 393.

limits of what Adams deemed America's legitimate interests.

Thus "the question which arose as a distinctly European question was changed into an American matter."[1] Once the message had been delivered Monroe himself was perfectly clear concerning the implications involved.

"By taking the step here," he wrote to Jefferson, "it is done in a manner more conciliatory with and respectful to Russia and the other powers, than if taken in England, and as it is thought with more credit to our government. Had we moved in the first instance in England, separated as she is in part from those powers, our union with her, being marked, might have produced irritation with them. We know that Russia dreads a connection between the United States and Great Britain or harmony in policy. Moving on our own ground the apprehension that unless she retreats, that effect may be produced may be a motive with her for retreating. Had we moved in England it is probable that it would have been inferred that we acted under her influence and at her instigation, and thus have lost credit as well with our southern neighbours as with the allied powers."[2]

"The message," wrote Addington to Canning, "seems to have been received with acclamation throughout the United States. The explicit and manly tone, especially, with which the President

[1] Ford, *American Historical Review*, Vol. VII., p. 676.
[2] Jefferson's MSS., *American Historical Review*, Vol. VIII., p. 51.

has treated the subject of European interference in the affairs of this hemisphere with a view to the subjugation of those territories which have emancipated themselves from European domination, has evidently found in every bosom a chord which vibrates in strict unison with the sentiments so conveyed. They have been echoed from one end of the Union to the other."

On the whole Great Britain found the Doctrine distinctly useful to her commercial interests. During the nineteenth century the South American States continued in close political and economic relations with the United States and Britain. The Anglo-Saxon markets absorbed their products, and loans from London and New York enabled them to develop their resources. Two thousand million pounds for investment have been poured into South America from these two cities alone. And though the rivalry between England and America has been intense, the bitterness of the last century has to a large extent been mitigated by more recent events. During the last century England's position was the stronger in South America, her investments were greater and her trade more important. With the turn of the century, however, the United States held the predominant position. Moreover, the feeling of kinship with Latin America has grown stronger, and the attempt to understand her southern neighbours has brought about a general feeling of harmony in ideals. Americans " cherish more vigorously than ever the ideal of free men to govern themselves according to their own free will." [1] But let there be no mistake, " The impulse of self protection remains the chief support of the doctrine." [1] The defence of the Panama Canal, the repercussions of German and Italian ideas in South America where they have been able to play an important part in politics, the position and power of Japan in the Pacific : all these factors, to name only the most important, have given the doctrine a new lease of life which is not likely to be snuffed out : a new significance which it would be unwise to ignore.

[1] *New York Times*, December 11, 1938. Alan Nevins.

Chapter VII

THE MESSAGE BECOMES DOCTRINE

The immediate effect of Monroe's message upon Europe was unimpressive. The continental Powers paid it little attention and England formally repudiated it. Canning, indeed, was fully alive to the implications involved and never lost an opportunity to limit its action, and, if possible, to discredit the United States.[1]

The South American States hailed it at first as a further assurance of their independence from the Spanish yoke, but during the next quarter of a century they were well aware that England, not the United States, was the powerful and interested protector against European adventurers.

Moreover, between 1823 and 1841 the interest in European systems was still considerable. In Mexico a strong monarchist party was working to replace Republican Government by a Bourbon king supported by Spain and possibly France. After an abortive attempt in 1829 the enterprise came to nothing. But it is apparent that the European Powers had not abandoned the idea of establishing their system in America.

[1] Perkins, *op. cit.*, p. 251.

THE MONROE DOCTRINE AND WORLD PEACE

On several occasions both the American and the British Governments behaved exactly as though the message had never been pronounced at all. And as several of the alleged violations occur during this period, they can be briefly reviewed here. When the British occupied the Falkland Islands in 1833, there was no representation to the Foreign Office from Washington, although it could have been assumed that the doctrine had been violated. The American Government refused to take the view that any American interest was involved.

When the British expanded their interests and activities at Belize in Central America between 1835 and 1838, the matter was brought to the attention of the State Department by the Central Americans themselves. They were told that " it was not deemed expedient to interfere in the matter."

When the French established a military port in territory claimed by Brazil in 1835, it was not the Government at Washington but the Government in London which brought enough pressure to bear on the French to effect a settlement.

When the French blockaded Mexico in 1838 and Vera Cruz was temporarily occupied, the American Government offered its assistance " in any form in which it may appear likely to appear beneficial," but Monroe's message was not referred to nor any Doctrine invoked, except for a resolution (February 11, 1838) brought into Congress by Caleb Cushing of Massachusetts in

THE MESSAGE BECOMES DOCTRINE

which Monroe's words were mentioned in a long preamble.

But the resolution committed the Government to nothing, and it was the British representative in Mexico, Richard Pakenham, whose skilful diplomacy brought the dispute to an end in 1839.

Other incidents could be added to these to show that not once during the period between 1826-41 " was the Doctrine invoked by those responsible for the conduct of the foreign policy of the United States. As a basis of action it was ignored completely and unequivocally." [1]

But during the next ten years there was a radical change in the public as well as the official attitude. In fact it can be said that until the forties Monroe's message, though not entirely forgotten, cannot be regarded as doctine at all. There are a number of reasons for this change; chief among them the portentous rise of nationalism in the country, the westward expansion, and the fevered intrigues of the European Powers to create and control the Balance of Power on the American continent.

After all, the Falkland Islands had been a long way off—even Central America and Mexico had had far less to do with American enterprise than with British capital. But as the pioneers drove their covered wagons ever westward, as the great Yankee clippers fought southward around the Horn, a new menace to American expansion appeared in British and French designs in Texas, in California, and in Oregon. Where could a

[1] *Op. cit.*, p. 59.

THE MONROE DOCTRINE AND WORLD PEACE

policy be found that would be positive and protective? Where but in the Presidential message of 1823.

During the revolt of Texas against Mexico in 1836 Palmerston declared in the House of Commons that America could not be allowed " to pursue a system of aggrandisement." When the treaty of annexation was discussed in 1843-44 British hostility to the project was apparent, and in 1844 Lord Aberdeen, the Foreign Secretary, appeared for a time to wish to make the Texas question a trial by war. But in Texas itself there was an irresistible tide of public opinion toward annexation to the United States, and the various attempts by British diplomats were abortive. The one result of the British efforts was to confirm American opinion in its belief that British diplomacy " paid not the slightest heed to any claim of special dominance which the United States had ever put forward, and that it was in fact hostile to the expansion, and in this case the peaceful expansion of the American people." [1]

But even more important than British hostility, which was after all traditional and accepted, was the knowledge that both Britain and France were attempting to impose a European Balance of Power on the American continent.

[1] The people of Texas still had a chance to choose between independence and union with the United States. The Texas Congress unanimously rejected the proposed treaty with Mexico (which England and France were urging), and when a Convention of the Republic met, July 4, 1845, it adopted an ordinance agreeing to annexation with only one dissenting voice. (Latané, *American Foreign Policy*, p. 258. Doubleday, Doran & Co., New York, 1934.)

THE MESSAGE BECOMES DOCTRINE

The Foreign Secretary declared [1] " that Her Majesty's Government are of opinion that the continuance of Texas as an independent Power under its own laws and institutions, must conduce to a more even, and therefore a more permanent balance of interests in the North American continent, and was the best chance of a preservation of friendly relations between those two Governments."

The French Prime Minister had made a similar declaration, and Americans were told in his speech that the interest of France in America " is that the independent States remain independent, that the balance of force between the great masses which divide America continue, that no one of them become exclusively preponderant. In America as in Europe, by the very fact that we have political and commercial interests we need independent States, a balance of power. This is the essential idea which ought to dominate France's American policy." [2]

Two other sources of suspicion helped to revive the Doctrine : Oregon and California, and in each case American suspicion was turned on Great Britain. Oregon had long been a matter of dispute. During 1844 the Doctrine was invoked in both Houses of Congress, and James K. Polk, the future President, wrote an open letter to the Press saying, " Let the fixed principle of our Government be not to permit Great Britain, or any other foreign power, to

[1] June 23, 1845.
[2] *Histoire Parlementaire de France*, Paris, 1867, Vol. IV., p. 562.

plant a colony or hold dominion over any portion of the people or territory of either continent." [1]

The third cause for the revival of the Doctrine was suspicion of Britain's designs on California. As far as the London Government was concerned these suspicions were largely unfounded, but British agents in Mexico and along the Pacific Coast did think seriously of the acquisition of the province by Great Britain. Thus Pakenham, the British Minister to Mexico, wrote to Lord Aberdeen: "I believe there is no part of the world offering greater natural advantages for the establishment of an English colony than the province of Upper California; while its commanding position on the Pacific, its fine harbours, its forests of excellent timber for shipbuilding, as well as for every other purpose, appear to me to render it by all means desirable, in a political point of view, that California, once ceasing to belong to Mexico should not fall into the hands of any Power but England, and the gradual increase of foreign population in California render it probable that its separation from Mexico will be effected at no distant period." [2]

Other agents were equally sure that California should be made a British protectorate, and enough was known by the corresponding American agents to arouse serious alarm in Washington.

Although not favouring an aggressive policy on the Pacific Coast, Aberdeen did go so far as

[1] *Washington Globe*, May 6, 1844.
[2] Public Record Office, London, F.O. 146-91.

THE MESSAGE BECOMES DOCTRINE

to write to his agents : " It is however of importance to Great Britain, while declining to interfere herself, that California, if it should throw off the Mexican yoke, should not assume any other which might prove inimical to British interests." [1]

In the face of these menaces, real and imagined, the idea of restating the principles laid down by Monroe was brought up in the Cabinet by Polk, who had recently been elected President on a platform which favoured annexation of Texas. Polk was a strong, narrow, stubborn man, uncritical, courageous, and patriotic. Just twenty years after Monroe's message to Congress he announced the same policy in a similar vigorous message, actually quoting the passage dealing with " future colonization " by any European Powers.

According to the greatest authority on the history of the doctrine, Polk's declaration " was beyond all doubt the most important single document intended to give renewed and greater weight to Monroe's principles between the date of the original message and the despatch of Secretary of State Richard Olney of June 20, 1895." [2]

The effect of this reiteration of the message is singular. Upon the Oregon question it had none whatever ; the dispute was finally settled the following year by a compromise treaty which, though favourable to the United States, did not

[1] Adams, *British Interests and Activities in Texas*, p. 248.
[2] Perkins, *The Monroe Doctrine, 1826–1867*, p. 89.

depend in the least upon any Doctrine. The *London Morning Chronicle* and the *Times* devoted sarcastic leading articles to Mr. Polk's message, declaring that it was dangerous to peace.

" If America is a world of its own, then also is each of the four conventional quarters of the globe," wrote the *Times* leader writer. " In fact there is no more reason in nature why America should segregate itself from the universal system and universal code than any other quarter. Nor does history present any contradiction to this antecedent and natural unity of the whole world. And the President only shows the utter groundlessness of his theory when he affects a reference to the political facts of the question. As a matter of fact nothing can be more untrue. By the proof of history America is inextricably mixed up with European politics." [1]

In France the message and the principles involved were even more severely condemned and directly challenged by the French Prime Minister Guizot. Not only did he repeat his ideas about the Balance of Power, he wrote to his Minister in Washington: " We refuse to admit those distinctions between American and European governments, between monarchies and republics. All civilized nations exist on the same legal basis and are equally obliged to respect one another."

Both England and France professed to see in the revival of the Monroe Message a doctrine which would serve conveniently for American expansion. Yet the Texas question was settled

[1] *Times*, December 27, 1845.

THE MESSAGE BECOMES DOCTRINE

peacefully according to the will of the Texans; the Oregon question, as we have seen, was adjusted by compromise; and the vast region of California and New Mexico was conquered by a few hundred men under General Kearney and Commodore Stockton, shortly after the outbreak of the war with Mexico.

Without doubt the statement of the Doctrine at this exciting period did serve a definite purpose. American distrust of European intervention was instinctive. If England had been successful in preventing the annexation of Texas, if she had persuaded France to join her at the same time as she provoked war with the United States, it is not unlikely that she would have succeeded in controlling the entire Pacific Coast from Alaska to Lower California. Polk's message centralized American determination to prevent such measures. Confronted by a belligerent America, France receded, Britain temporized, and Mexico was left to her own embroiled and stupid conduct of affairs.

Chapter VIII

MEXICAN ADVENTURE [1]

" There will not be lacking people who will ask why we are going to spend men and money to place an Austrian prince upon a throne [in Mexico]." [2] In these words Louis Napoleon began his explanation of the bizarre and romantic escapade of Archduke Maximilian, Emperor of Mexico, which came to an abrupt and tragic end before a firing squad at dawn, June 19, 1867, five years and sixteen days later, largely because of the intervention of the Monroe Doctrine.

" In the actual state of the civilization of the world " continued the Emperor of the French, " the prosperity of America is not indifferent to Europe, for it nourishes our industry and gives life to our commerce. We are interested in seeing

[1] Only the most important crisis in which the Doctrine has been invoked can come within the scope of this discussion. For a detailed account of every instance relating to Monroe's Message the reader is referred to the three volumes by Professor Dexter Perkins which constitute the standard work on the subject. As a scholarly analysis of the development of the Doctrine they are unsurpassed. Mr. E. H. Tatum's study of the causes and origins is also indispensable, and Professor J. Fred Rippy's researches upon Anglo-American and Latin-American relations are both enlightening and outstanding. I am deeply indebted to these three scholars for their permission to quote from their works.

[2] July 3, 1862.

the United States powerful and prosperous, but we have no interest in seeing that republic acquire the whole of the Gulf of Mexico, dominate from this vantage-point the Antilles and South America, and become the sole dispenser of the products of the New World, mistress of Mexico and consequently of Central America and of the passage between the two seas. There would be henceforth no other power in America than the United States.

" If, on the other hand, Mexico conquers its independence and maintains the integrity of its territory, if a stable government is constituted there by the arms of France, we shall have opposed an insuperable barrier to the encroachments of the United States, we shall have maintained the independence of our colonies in the Antilles and of those of ungrateful Spain, and we shall have established our beneficent influence in the centre of America, and this influence will radiate northward as well as southward, will create immense markets for our commerce, and will procure the materials indispensable to our industry." [1]

A brief account of the causes which led to this extraordinary and hostile declaration is necessary in order to understand how the Doctrine and the Emperor became involved with each other.

For forty years or more the relations between the United States and Mexico had been stormy, to say the least. Mexico had always been fiercely anti-American. As recently as 1853 both the

[1] July 3, 1862. *Documents Diplomatic*, 1863.

THE MONROE DOCTRINE AND WORLD PEACE

Press and the Government had made appeals to Europe for help against the domination of the Anglo-Saxons. In Mexico City the fear of the United States was shared by the European diplomats. "Only Europe can save Mexico," wrote the French minister (August 1, 1853). Added to the menace of American oppression was the chaotic state of Mexico itself. Régime succeeded régime with bewildering speed accompanied by shootings, border raids, and financial chaos. There was more than sufficient argument for intervention to compose the differences between the warring factions. In August 1860 a proposal for common action by France, Great Britain, Spain, and the United States reached Washington. The Americans refused, and President Buchanan stated the American point of view.

" The United States had determined to resist any forcible attempt to impose a particular adjustment of the existing conflict against the will and sanction of the people of Mexico, and also any forcible intervention by any power which looks to the control of the political destiny thereof." [1]

The following year conditions in Mexico became worse, and the patience of the European Powers was exhausted. The British Embassy in Mexico City was robbed of over £100,000 by Government agents, private property was at the mercy of bandits, commerce and trade were at a standstill. Spain and France had grievances as well as Great Britain—the Civil War had burst

[1] December, 1860.

upon the United States, and there was no likelihood of opposition from that quarter for the time being. Intervention by the three Powers was decided upon at the Convention of London, October 30, 1861.

It was to be a restrained intervention to restore order, to allow the country to organize itself, and, of course, to control the customs until various claims were settled. Moreover, the Convention undertook not to interfere with " the right of the Mexican Government to choose and to constitute freely its own form of government."

But already Louis Napoleon was dreaming of establishing an empire in Mexico with a prince of his own choice for ruler, and the inexhaustible mines of gold and silver to pay the dividends on his dreams.

From the very beginning the wild affair did not appeal to English good sense, and Lord John Russell, the Foreign Secretary, made it clear that Britain did not look upon the scheme with any favour. In his view the intervention should be restricted, and the United States should not be antagonized. The British Government " could never recognize what was commonly called the Monroe Doctrine," but at the same time it was not expedient to arouse American feeling by appearing to infringe even " an imagined right." This cautious realism remained British policy throughout the affair. If the Mexican people really desired monarchy and Maximilian, Britain could scarcely take objection, but Lord John doubted whether they really did. From the

THE MONROE DOCTRINE AND WORLD PEACE

American point of view this was in pleasant contrast to the Texas-California affair, and no sinister or ulterior motives can be laid against British policy.

Louis Napoleon, on the other hand, was eager to checkmate the rise of American power and influence; he was avowedly hostile, and he saw in the disorganization of Mexico a field ripe for his purpose. Spain was prepared to support him in his schemes. The Civil War made American intervention impossible for the time being, and nothing remained save to choose the leaders and the time. Neither France nor Spain believed that any effective resistance would be offered in Mexico itself.

The Mexican adventure opened with an allied intervention by Spain, Britain, and France. The object was the regeneration of Mexico, but the motives were distinctly mixed, and led to dissension among the Allies from the very beginning. By April 1862 Britain had withdrawn to the side lines. The Spanish representative, General Prin, was reluctant to antagonize America, which, in his opinion, would apply the Doctrine as soon as the Civil War was over. Louis Napoleon was left practically alone with his favourite idea of Maximilian and Monarchy. In the summer of 1863 French troops entered Mexico City, and during the winter of 1864 the Archduke was approached at his castle of Miramar by French and Mexican emissaries, and he accepted the proffered throne on April 10, 1864. Austria, on the other hand, kept aloof and viewed

MEXICAN ADVENTURE

the affair with scepticism. For behind all the intrigues and hopes of Louis Napoleon, behind the dreams of the puppet emperor at Miramar rose the formidable battalions of the army of the Potomac and the warning of American ministers in Europe that American feeling against such an enterprize would be " universal and intense."

From the American point of view Louis Napoleon's adventure in Mexico was the most serious attack on the Monroe Doctrine that has ever occurred, and it did more to lift the principles declared by Monroe above party politics and enshrine them as truly national principles than any other crisis before or since.

President Lincoln's Secretary of State Seward handled this important matter with admirable circumspection. From the beginning he made the American position perfectly clear. As early as March 2, 1862, he sent a dispatch to Charles Francis Adams, the American minister in London, stating in unequivocal but suave language the principles of the Monroe Doctrine. But he did not mention the Doctrine by name. He knew that Europe was hostile to it, and that Europe must not be unduly irritated while the Civil War lasted. But underneath the diplomatic phrases he made it evident that America would oppose any " armed intervention for political ends in a country situated so near and connected so closely as Mexico."

Seward was faced with the most difficult task imaginable. His impetuosity led him toward a

THE MONROE DOCTRINE AND WORLD PEACE

bold anti-French policy, but his statesmanship councilled him to moderation. " Why," he wrote to Bigelow in France, " should we gasconade about Mexico when we are in a struggle for our own life ? " [1]

The first seven months of the Civil War were the most critical for the Union. The Rebels were victorious in the field, they were known to have designs on Mexico, and in addition to these troubles Seward was presented with the *fait accompli* of European intervention. It would be impossible to overrate his conduct in the face of these perplexities. He never retreated from his position that the French armed intervention was contrary to the Doctrine and harmful to the interests of the United States; but he adopted a tone of moderation to such effect that Napoleon was never given a cause to strike at the Union when it was going through evil days. Seward was firmly convinced that the Mexican question could be solved without war with France. As the Civil War turned in favour of the Federal Government a growing feeling of indignation and hostility to Napoleon's adventure developed in America. " Drive the French out of Mexico," became a popular slogan. As the war came to an end Napoleon's enthusiasm for Maximilian and Mexico became considerably modified. Rumours began to reach Paris that the victorious army would throw itself upon Mexico as soon as the war was over. And, indeed, after Lee's surrender at Appomatox there were active plans for

[1] Bancroft, *Seward*, Vol. II., p. 430.

MEXICAN ADVENTURE

Generals Grant, Sheridan, and Schofield to lead a force against the French. The people were demanding a more vigorous policy for the vindication of the Monroe Doctrine. With this public clamour behind him Seward adopted a threatening tone in his dispatches to Paris of July 6, 1865. By December, Napoleon had come to the conclusion that his puppet Emperor was not worth a war with the United States and that withdrawal from the adventure was the only way out. Moreover, Prussia was causing him anxiety in Europe, and the unpleasant reports from his officers in Mexico added to his embarrassment. At this propitious moment Seward pressed his diplomatic advantage and Napoleon abandoned his protégé, his Mexican empire, and his dreams of checkmating America. The last French troops were withdrawn on March 12, 1867. It was indeed an overwhelming victory for the Monroe Doctrine.

The subsequent history of the ill-fated adventure does not concern us here. Seward attempted to intervene with the Mexican Indian leader, Juarez, in behalf of the helpless Maximilian. But the relentless Mexican ignored the diplomatic approaches of a race he despised and feared, and Maximilian faced the firing squad at Guéretaro on the morning of June 19, 1867.[1]

[1] Works consulted in connection with this chapter: Rippy, *The United States and Mexico*; Corti, *Maximilian and Charlotte of Mexico*, New York, 1926; besides volumes already referred to.

Chapter IX

THE PANAMA CANAL

BETWEEN the evacuation of the French from Mexico and the opening of the famous dispute over the Venezuela boundary, the Doctrine figured in a number of relatively unimportant diplomatic manœuvres for the possesssion or the transference of several of the West Indian Islands. Whenever the shadow of a European Power was detected falling across the Caribbean, American sensitiveness appeared to grow, rather than diminish; though it is fair to point out that in spite of a general principle of no transfer (added by Hamilton Fish the Secretary of State in 1870) America did nothing when presented with the *fait accompli* of the transfer of the island of St. Bartholomew from Sweden to France in 1877. However, it became apparent to Europeans as well as to Americans that Caribbean expansion, already a favourite ambition before the Civil War, was now beginning to revive with a new vigour as the nation recovered its unity and strength.

During the discussions over the Panama Canal it was inevitable that the Doctrine should be invoked. As early as 1826 the American dele-

THE PANAMA CANAL

gates at the Congress of Panama were instructed to approach the question.[1] Leaving aside the endless negotiations, there remain three important treaties up to 1900 which implicated the United States in the question of a canal across the isthmus. (1) The Columbia Treaty of 1846; (2) the Clayton-Bulwer Treaty with Britain, 1850; (3) the Nicaragua Treaty of 1867. Under the first treaty the neutrality of the isthmus was asserted, the treaty to last for twenty years. Shortly after this treaty Americans constructed the Panama railway across the isthmus.

The Clayton-Bulwer Treaty, which gave rise to years of discussion and invocation of the Doctrine, was, in brief, a declaration by the United States and Britain that neither should obtain exclusive rights over the canal (if and when built), and that in case of war between the contracting parties the canal should be neutralized. It was fiercely criticized at the time and for many years afterward. President Buchanan himself declared that, "if Sir Henry Bulwer can succeed in having the two first provisions of this treaty ratified by the Senate, he will deserve a British peerage."

But this treaty, which was to cause such bitterness and recrimination, was not without some justification. Britain was in possession of the Atlantic entrance to the proposed canal. America had no treaty rights with Nicaragua. If England's evident desire to expand and eventually to control the isthmus were to be counteracted at

[1] Latané, *American Foreign Policy*, p. 309.

all, there was at this time nothing for America to adopt save the Monroe Doctrine. The only false move on the American side was the exclusion of any time limit or clause of abrogation. This, as we shall see, gave the British the chance for a certain amount of superior diplomatic back chat and acid moralizing on the *status quo*; but the outcome was a new agreement establishing the American point of view, that the canal must be a part of the American political and defence system.

On March 8, 1880, President Hayes announced the new American policy toward the Canal question.

" The policy of this country," he said, " is a canal under American control. The United States cannot consent to the surrender of their control to any European power, or to any combination of European powers. If existing treaties between the United States and other nations, or if the rights of sovereignty or property of other nations stand in the way of this policy— a contingency which is not apprehended—suitable steps should be taken by just and liberal negotiations to promote and establish the American policy on this subject, consistently with the rights of the nations to be affected by it."

" The canal," concluded the President, " will be the great ocean thoroughfare between our Atlantic and our Pacific shores, and virtually a part of the coast-line of the United States."

From the American point of view all moves in the Canal question must lead to a new agreement.

THE PANAMA CANAL

But this agreement was not arrived at without a great deal of diplomatic wrangling in which England held by far the superior position. For Lord Granville pointed out, when presented with the American policy, " that the matter in question had already been settled by the engagements of the Clayton-Bulwer Treaty and that Her Majesty's Government relied with confidence upon the observation of all the obligations of that treaty."

The American Secretary of State, Blaine, found himself embarrassed. Public opinion in favour of an American controlled canal was assuming overwhelming impetus. The immense development of the West seemed to offer a new argument, and Blaine invoked the Doctrine as doubly justifying the change of attitude; but, as Granville took pains to emphasize in a withering answer, the Clayton-Bulwer treaty was concluded twenty-seven years after Monroe's message and the Government and Congress which sanctioned it did not consider that " they were precluded by the utterances of President Monroe in 1823 from entering into such a treaty with one or more of the European powers."

England refused to admit the American change of policy, and in 1896 Secretary Olney declared that the only method of solving the question was in a direct and straightforward application to Great Britain for a reconsideration of the whole matter. The Venezuela crisis (which will be considered separately) intervened; but finally, in 1901, Secretary of State Hay concluded a treaty with Lord Pauncefote abrogating the Clayton-

THE MONROE DOCTRINE AND WORLD PEACE

Bulwer convention and leaving the United States free to build, police, and protect the Panama Canal.

During the long years of controversy over this most important matter it became increasingly evident that the famous Doctrine was taking deeper roots in the feelings of the American people, and it is not exaggerated to claim that it played a large, if indeterminate, part in the final settlement with Britain.

But before this settlement had been reached, America and England had been through the Venezuela crisis, the last serious dispute between the two countries in which the Doctrine played a deciding part, a dispute which produced the singular phenomena of more cordial feelings than had ever existed before in Anglo-American relations and "initiated a virtual *entente* that within a generation was to prove of the profoundest importance in world history." [1]

It is also interesting to remark that a second Venezuela crisis a few years later [2] brought Germany into conflict with the Doctrine and helped to produce a shifting in the balance of world politics that had the most momentous results in 1914. For there is no respite for nations any more than for the men who compose them. Political relationships must either move or cease to exist. The *status quo* is a figment of the dreams of those who have—hoping that they can keep it, often forgetting how they won it, and persuading others not by any means to go and do likewise.

[1] Nevins, *Grover Cleveland*, p. 648.　　[2] 1902.

CHAPTER X

THE FIRST VENEZUELA CRISIS, 1895

THE first Venezuela crisis brought England and America to the verge of war ; it gave Europe a sudden and unpleasant realization of the full power of the American dogma ; and it "placed the principles of 1823 on a new pinnacle of regard in the United States."[1]

Nothing in the past ever aroused such universal hostility to the United States as this incident, and it is a striking instance of what the Secretary of State Olney termed the patriotism of race, that it was in England itself that moderation and good sense prevailed to a remarkable degree.

The dispute arose over the question of the boundary line between Venezuela and British Guiana. It had remained unsettled since 1814, when Britain came into possession of what had been Dutch territory. Venezuela claimed the line of the Essequibo River. Britain established a line known as the Schomburgk line drawn by Sir Robert Schomburgk in 1840. Since then Venezuela claimed, with some justice, that the line had varied several times, always in favour of Britain (see, for example, the British Colonial

[1] Perkins, *The Monroe Doctrine, 1867–1907*, p. 252.

THE MONROE DOCTRINE AND WORLD PEACE

Office list for changes in the size of the territory). Venezuela urged Britain to settle the matter by arbitration, and after persistent refusals she broke off diplomatic relations in 1887 and appealed to Washington for help.

Some years were to pass before the Venezuela boundary question grew into a major crisis. The early exchanges of diplomatic notes were polite and unhurried. Certainly at this time President Cleveland did not foresee anything more than a friendly settlement. He offered to bring about a restoration of relations between the two countries, and instructed his Ambassador in London, Bayard, to approach the Government with a view to reaching an honourable conclusion. But it became evident that the British Government were determined not to arbitrate.[1] Moreover, in the spring of 1895 a number of other influences began to make themselves felt. The American Press was referring to "British Aggression in Venezuela, or the Monroe Doctrine on Trial." The *New York Tribune* [2] wrote that " the Doctrine is as pertinent and important in 1895 as it was in 1823." The *Telegram* declared that " England, France and Germany may yet have to be diplomatically informed that the Monroe Doctrine has never been abrogated." The *Chicago Tribune* wrote that " the United States under the Monroe Doctrine could never look on complacently at such an absorption of Venezuelan territory." And other leading papers echoed the same sentiments.

[1] April 5, 1895. [2] March 23rd.

THE FIRST VENEZUELA CRISIS, 1895

Henry Cabot Lodge, the young Senator from Massachusetts, delivered himself of a fiery appeal ending with the words, " The supremacy of the Monroe Doctrine should be established and at once—peaceably if we can, forcibly if we must. It will be the duty and the privilege of the next Congress to see that this is done."[1] Lodge was warmly congratulated by his friend Theodore Roosevelt. England remained blandly indifferent to the growing irritation in America.

Meanwhile Richard Olney, the new Secretary of State, was preparing a remarkable dispatch for Bayard in London. His chief, President Cleveland, a slow-moving, resolute man, had finally decided to take a firm stand and if necessary force a settlement by arbitration. For many years the British Government had shown not the slightest interest in the American suggestions, and had in fact behaved with a languid and supercilious indifference which was intensely irritating to a man of Olney's " harsh and imperious temper."

The famous dispatch of July 20, 1895, was chiefly concerned with the bearing of the Monroe Doctrine upon the Venezuela question. After stating what he considered to be the salient points of the controversy, Olney wrote :

" By the frequent interposition of its good offices at the instance of Venezuela, by constantly urging and promoting the restoration of diplomatic relations between the two countries, by pressing for arbitration of the disputed

[1] *North American Review*, Vol. CLX., p. 658.

THE MONROE DOCTRINE AND WORLD PEACE

boundary, by offering to act as arbitrator, by expressing its grave concern whenever new alleged instances of British aggression upon Venezuelan territory have been brought to its notice, the Government of the United States has made it clear to Great Britain and to the world that the controversy is one in which both its honour and its interests are involved and the continuance of which it cannot regard with indifference."

Olney's reference to the Doctrine deserves to be quoted in full:

"That America is in no part open to colonization though the proposition was not universally admitted at the time of its first enunciation, has long been universally conceded. We are now concerned, therefore, only with that other practical application of the Monroe Doctrine, the disregard of which by a European power is to be deemed an act of unfriendliness toward the United States.

"The precise scope and limitations of this rule cannot be too clearly apprehended. It does not establish any general protectorate by the United States over other American states. It does not relieve any American state from its obligations as fixed by international law nor prevent any European power directly interested from enforcing such obligations or from inflicting merited punishment for the breach of them. It does not contemplate any interference in the internal affairs of any American state, or in the relations between it and any other American

THE FIRST VENEZUELA CRISIS, 1895

state. It does not justify any attempt on our part to change the established form of government of any American state or to prevent the people of such a state from altering that form according to their own will and pleasure. The rule in question has but a single purpose and object. It is that no European power or combination of European powers shall forcibly deprive an American state of the right and power of self-government and of shaping for itself its own political fortunes and destinies."

Many of the paragraphs, however, went far beyond these moderate generalizations. Olney dwelt with complacency on the differences between the American and European political systems. He asserted that British acquisition of some thousands of square miles of swamp and wilderness constituted a first-class menace to American security, and he maintained that the distance between Europe and America made any close union unnatural and inexpedient. Besides these extremely questionable assertions, Olney declared that the question of the settlement involved " a doctrine of American public law, well founded in principle and abundantly sanctioned by precedent, which entitles the United States to treat as an injury to itself the forcible assumption by a European power of political control over an American state."

The conclusion of the dispatch was in the nature of an ultimatum. It was perfectly clear to any one who chose to read that the American Government was prepared to uphold their inter-

THE MONROE DOCTRINE AND WORLD PEACE

pretation of the Doctrine by force if necessary. Either England would submit to arbitration or she would have to accept the challenge.

Olney's note of 20th July was read to Lord Salisbury by the American Ambassador, Mr. Thomas Bayard, on 7th August. Lord Salisbury's first reaction was " regret and surprise that it had been considered necessary to present so far-reaching and important a principle and such wide and profound policies of international action in relation to a subject so comparatively small."

In any case he was not inclined to hurry, and not until 26th November did he conclude his answer.

Instead of cabling it he sent it by post, so that it arrived too late for the opening of Congress. The long delay in answering had already caused a storm in the Press and in official circles, and the casual manner of transmission only led to further irritation. Nor was Salisbury's reply calculated to ease the situation. He flatly denied that the Monroe Doctrine could claim to be an article of International Law, and challenged Olney's interference. His tone was peremptory and dogmatic. A number of Olney's statements were easily answered. Salisbury made fun of the phrase " unnatural and inexpedient " and pointed to Canada, Jamaica, Trinidad, and Guiana.

The answer was undoubtedly able, and it produced President Cleveland's message to Congress of 17th December.

Cleveland did not reply to Salisbury's discussion of the Doctrine, he flatly asserted that

THE FIRST VENEZUELA CRISIS, 1895

America stood upon it and would act accordingly. He proposed that Congress appoint a Committee to investigate the merits of the boundary dispute, and declared that the matter would be settled by arbitration upon that report.

"When such report is made and accepted," concluded the President, "it will in my opinion be the duty of the United States to resist by every means in its power as a wilful aggression upon its rights and interests the appropriation by Great Britain of any lands or the exercise of governmental jurisdiction over any territory which after investigation we have determined of right belongs to Venezuela.

"In making these recommendations I am fully alive to the responsibility incurred and keenly realize all the consequences that may follow."

The reaction of Congress was highly favourable, and a storm of praise echoed throughout the country. But there was fierce criticism as well. The pulpit, the Bar, and the universities raised powerful voices—objecting to the tone of the message, to the logic upon which it was based, and above all to the idea of going to war with England over an undefined wilderness.

In England there was also considerable feeling. The *St. James's Gazette* wanted to know, "what this blessed Monroe Doctrine really is and why it should be drawn into a dispute between Britain and a third power." But whereas in America a wave of nationalism followed Cleveland's speech, there was no such counter reaction in Great Britain. The British public knew very little

THE MONROE DOCTRINE AND WORLD PEACE

about Venezuela, and as the great James Bryce explained in an article, a large part of that public was frankly bewildered to find so much hostility in America. Indeed, there was a surprising amount of English opinion in favour of accepting President Cleveland's arbitration commission. The Prince of Wales and his son, the Duke of York, took the unprecedented step of expressing themselves publicly on the side of arbitration. " They earnestly trust and can but believe the present crisis will be arranged in a manner satisfactory to both countries, and will be succeeded by the same warm feeling of friendship which has existed between them for so many years." [1]

Scarcely less influential in forming British opinion were Joseph Chamberlain and Sir William Harcourt, both of whom were married to American wives and both of whom worked whole-heartedly for conciliation.

There were, of course, other factors which contributed to change the didactic attitude of Lord Salisbury. There was a vast amount of English capital in America, there was also a greater understanding among the people, and as Professor Perkins points out, it is fair to ask whether " it had not become extremely difficult for the British masses to envisage with complacency a war with the United States, with its similar instinct for democracy, its common language and its ties of blood."

[1] Telegram from H.R.H.'s secretary to the *New York World*, Christmas Day, 1895.

THE FIRST VENEZUELA CRISIS, 1895

Thus, unexpectedly, the truculence of Olney, the popular invocation of the Doctrine by Cleveland, and the provocative dogmatizing of Salisbury led to more cordial expressions of Anglo-American friendship than for many years past. By February 1896 Salisbury himself was declaring in Parliament that American interference " may conduce to results which will be satisfactory to us more rapidly than if the United States had not interfered." [1]

Cleveland himself never moved from the position he had taken up and remained entirely undisturbed by the criticism of his policy. His diplomatic move turned out to be a complete success. The boundary line was arbitrated according to the findings of the commission appointed by Congress. And even before the final report had been submitted, there was a complete accord between the two governments which led to the proposal of a treaty of general arbitration. The treaty between Great Britain and Venezuela was signed in Washington, February 2, 1897, and the final negotiations were concluded in the autumn of 1899. A large part of the disputed area went to Great Britain ; two parts within the Schomburgk line were awarded to Venezuela. But the result was not so important as the principle involved. Great Britain had agreed to arbitrate and had recognized in practice the United States claim to intervene. America had become aware that she had responsibilities overseas ; and finally, when

[1] *Hansard*, Vol. XXXVII., c. 52.

THE MONROE DOCTRINE AND WORLD PEACE

shortly afterward Germany questioned the American dogma, it became evident that there was a new Balance of Power rising in the twentieth century which can be partially accounted for by the friendly settlement of the first Venezuela crisis.

There are one or two more points to be considered in this brief review of a famous incident. Both England and America were at the beginning of a period of intense nationalistic feeling; both were about to undertake imperialist wars, America against Spain, England against the Boers. During the first flare-up over the Venezuela question, and while the intense feelings provoked by Cleveland's message [1] were at their height, the Jameson Raid occurred and the Kaiser sent his telegram of congratulations to President Kruger.[2] How far Salisbury was influenced by the state of affairs in South Africa is open to conjecture; but what is perfectly plain is the fact that British reaction to the German gesture was violent and unequivocally belligerent, whereas to the American gesture it had been annoyed, but on the whole conciliatory.[3]

---

[1] December 17, 1895.   [2] January 3, 1896.

[3] On January 15, 1896, two weeks after the Kaiser's telegram, Balfour referred to the Monroe Doctrine in a speech at Manchester. He declared that "a statesman of greater authority even than Monroe will lay down the Doctrine that between English-speaking peoples war is impossible."

Chapter XI

THE SECOND VENEZUELA CRISIS

When on April 21, 1898, the United States and Spain went to war, there had been intense diplomatic action in Europe to form a coalition of Powers strong enough to prevent the outbreak. Austria had attempted to organize an allied front on Spain's behalf. The German Kaiser had suggested at one point of the negotiations that all the European Powers should intervene in Cuba to prevent American aggression.[1] But the confused state of Europe and the assurance that England had no idea of taking drastic action made it sufficiently evident to M'Kinley's Administration that America could risk intervention with every chance of success. There was, in fact, a deep division of feeling between England and the Continental Powers over the Spanish war. Balfour and Chamberlain were outspoken in their support of America, and England generally sympathized, where the continental nations made no secret of their hostility and ill-will toward American expansion. As far as the Doctrine is concerned, it was not invoked by M'Kinley's Administration, and it cannot be called upon

[1] September 28, 1897.

THE MONROE DOCTRINE AND WORLD PEACE

either to condemn or to justify the intervention in Cuba or the annexation of the Philippines. It is true that some European writers gleefully exclaimed that the Monroe Doctrine was thrown overboard—but such opinions were little more than evidence of the ill-natured comment on America to be found in Europe at almost any time, and which was particularly violent in 1898.[1]

In America itself there were divided opinions over the Doctrine and annexation of the Pacific islands. Conservatives professed to see a glaring inconsistency in policy, while those favouring annexation were careful not to invoke the Doctrine in any form whatever. But the eventual annexation of the Philippines, Orian, Samoa, and Wake islands, completed by 1899, found the Doctrine still alive and prepared to resist the encroachment of a new world rival in Germany. It is interesting to remark that England consistently urged America to maintain the position she had won in the Pacific, and that both countries so long in dispute with each other realized simultaneously that the new Power in Europe would be a jealous and a bitter antagonist.

The growth of German power, the expansion of her political ambitions, and her rivalry and conflict with America and England would furnish material for a book far wider in scope than this discussion can allow. From the time when Bismarck was in power Germany had determined

[1] De Baumarchais, *La Doctrine de Monroe*, Paris 1898, Kraus; H. Pétin, *Les États-Unis et la doctrine de Monroe*.

THE SECOND VENEZUELA CRISIS

to challenge the Monroe Doctrine. Roosevelt, Lodge, Root, Hay, and other leading Americans already questioned her motives and distrusted her designs at the end of the Spanish-American war. She was supposed to have ambitions to possess harbours on the Venezuela coast; she had her eye on the Danish West Indies, Haiti, and the Dominican Republic. It is now evident that Germany really wanted more than anything else to prevent an Anglo-American understanding, but, as always, she misunderstood the Anglo-Saxon countries and drove the wedge with which she was preparing to divide them into her own flank.

Theodore Roosevelt's first message to Congress discussed the Doctrine in terms that were traditional and extremely conservative. The Doctrine was neither hostile to Europe nor to South America. The President defined the Doctrine as being against " territorial aggrandisement by any non-American power on American soil." He also made it clear to the South American republics that the United States was not a guarantor against punishment for misconduct. Even when he had been Vice-President he had made it clear that in his opinion, " If any South American country misbehaves toward any European country let the European country spank it." [1]

In 1902 this last observation led to an important episode in connection with the Monroe

[1] Roosevelt to the German Ambassador von Sternberg, July 12, 1901.

THE MONROE DOCTRINE AND WORLD PEACE

Doctrine. For three years Venezuela had been under the rule of a singularly unpleasant dictator by the name of Castro. Foreign interests in the country were considerable ; railways, mines, banks, and other enterprises amounting in the case of Germany alone to 180 million marks. England and America also had large stakes in the country, and it was generally recognized that something must be done to deal with Castro, who was defaulting on Government bonds, destroying foreign ships, and making it impossible for any orderly business to be carried on in the country. When the Germans first conceived the idea of using some form of chastisement to restore order they were well aware that they must move cautiously in order not to disturb their relations with the United States. The German Ambassador approached the State Department with a plan of action which included a blockade of Venezuelan ports, and, if necessary, an occupation, a temporary occupation, of certain harbours and customs.[1]

After carefully considering the matter the American Government saw no reason for objection, provided, of course, that the measures taken were purely temporary and not merely a cloak for more ambitious designs.

The British also had claims on Venezuela, and after long-drawn-out talks with the Germans it was decided to establish a joint blockade of Venezuelan ports. Neither country had any reason to fear American intervention. In fact,

[1] December 11, 1901.

THE SECOND VENEZUELA CRISIS

when the Secretary of State was approached by the British Ambassador with Lord Lansdowne's dispatch containing news of the British threat against Venezuela, he "stated in reply that the United States Government although they regretted that European powers should use force against Central and South American countries, could not object to their taking steps to obtain redress for injuries suffered by their subjects, provided that no acquisition of territory was contemplated."[1]

Such a reply could only be taken to mean that the Government at Washington fully concurred in the punitive measures contemplated by Germany and England. It is true that the Navy Department took the precaution to send a large fleet under Admiral Dewey to manœuvre in the West Indies, and that Roosevelt, always interested in the Navy, must have approved. But there is nothing to indicate that the administration was unduly disturbed by the prospect in the Caribbean during the autumn of 1902.

The punitive measures began on 9th December, and, as generally happens, did not proceed in as orderly fashion as might have been hoped. On the 9th the Germans seized some Venezuelan gunboats, and sank two of them. On the following day the British landed and evacuated their nationals; and on the 13th, in retaliation for insults to the British ship *Topaz*, British and German cruisers bombarded the forts of Puerto

[1] November 13, 1902. *British and Foreign State Papers*, Vol. XCV., 1901–2, pp. 1081–82.

Cabello. On 20th December the blockade was officially announced.

During these events, it is important to point out, there was no protest whatever from Washington. It was clear that the Government acquiesced in foreign intervention, although some observers noticed that public feeling was beginning to be aroused by the presence of European armed forces in the Caribbean. By the 16th, that is to say, four days before the official blockade had been established, both England and Germany had agreed in principle to an offer of arbitration transmitted by Castro through Washington. And in accepting this offer both countries appealed to Roosevelt to be the arbitrator. That it pleased the dramatic President is evident; but, considering that America was also an interested Power in the dispute, he adopted a cautious attitude and referred the matter to the Hague Tribunal. Meanwhile the blockade was put into force.

In England there were many indications that the policy of intervention was far from being approved. The Liberal party would have nothing to do with an alliance with Germany. The Opposition in the House was highly critical of any move which would arouse American hostility.[1]

On January 17, 1903, the German gunboat *Panther* bombarded Venezuelan ports. And in both the United States and Great Britain the criticism to this debt-collecting adventure grew stronger. Kipling had already written a poem,

Hansard, Vol. CXVI., 1902, pp. 1246–87.

THE SECOND VENEZUELA CRISIS

published in the *Times* of December 22, 1902, condemning the co-operation with Germany—Germany who had backed the Boers. Austen Chamberlain, Lord Cranborne, and others took occasion to point out that England would not dream of violating the Monroe Doctrine, and Lord Lansdowne took notice of the violent anti-German feeling and began to wish himself out of the adventure altogether. The Prime Minister Balfour, the Duke of Devonshire, and other influential men made it clear that the Venezuela policy in no way challenged the Doctrine, to which they avowed their unwavering support. Indeed, one of the most remarkable results of this new crisis was the widely expressed desire by English politicians to do nothing that could in any way infringe on the famous Doctrine. Berlin called it truckling, and would have none of it. But Berlin was wrong. England and the Doctrine both emerged from the blockade with better reputations than ever before. Germany, on the other hand, remained suspect. There were, it is true, various motives behind the English expression of allegiance to the Doctrine: England wanted one of two things—the right to intervene in the unruly South American republics if her interests were threatened, or the assurance that the United States would do so.

But this British policy, which was to blossom into a remarkable extension of the American Doctrine, did not meet with any acceptance when first proposed. In fact Admiral Mahan answered the British thesis in an article published in the

Review of Reviews and the *National Review* in March 1903. It is worth quoting as a criticism of the future Roosevelt corollary of an international police force.

"Not to invade the rights of an American state," wrote Mahan, "is to the United States an obligation with the force of law. To permit no European state to infringe them is a matter of policy: but as she will not acquiesce in any assault upon their independence or territorial integrity, so she will not countenance by her support any shirking of their international responsibility. Neither will she undertake to compel them to observe their international obligations to others than herself. To do so, which has been by some most inconsequently argued a necessary corollary of the Monroe Doctrine, would encroach on the very independence upon which that political dogma depends; for to assume the responsibility which derives from independence and can only be transferred by its surrender, would be to assert a quasi suzerainty.

"The United States is inevitably the preponderant American power: but she does not aspire to be paramount. She does not find the true complement to the Monroe Doctrine in an undefined control over American states, exercised by her and denied to Europe. Its correlative, as forcibly urged by John Quincy Adams at the time of formulation, is abstention from interference in questions territorially European."

The Venezuela episode was finally settled by arbitration. The blockade was lifted and the

THE SECOND VENEZUELA CRISIS

papers signed on February 13, 1903, pledging 30 per cent. of the customs toward payment of the various claims. But the really interesting result lay in the new relations between England, Germany, and the United States. The Doctrine emerged with " an immensely increased authority." England had put on record her whole-hearted acceptance, and it was felt generally that a new era of friendship between the two nations was beginning. Germany, on the other hand, had taken her place as the menacing Power. The American people had been stirred by German conduct, and the feeling against the blockade seemed to lay the blame, rightly or wrongly, on German methods and German truculence. Moreover, America herself was beginning to be conscious of her growing strength, and the vigour and assurance of her energetic President were indications that she was entering a new phase in her national development.

NOTE.—There is one dramatic incident in the Venezuela crisis which must be referred to with extreme caution.

According to various statements of President Roosevelt himself, Germany had been slow to accept the suggestion of arbitration and acute tension had developed between the Kaiser and America. Years later, in 1916, Roosevelt went so far as to declare that he had delivered an ultimatum to Germany saying that unless she agreed to arbitrate he would order Dewey and the American Fleet to the Venezuelan coast.

THE MONROE DOCTRINE AND WORLD PEACE

Dewey also published a letter saying that he had " orders from Washington to hold the fleet in hand and be ready to move at a moment's notice. Fortunately, however, the whole matter was amicably adjusted and there was no need for action."

On the day this letter was published Roosevelt made the following announcement from his house at Oyster Bay on Long Island :

" Just to-day I was very glad to see published in the papers the letter of Admiral Dewey describing an incident that took place when I was President. When we were menaced with trouble I acted up to my theory that the proper way of handling international relations was by speaking softly and carrying a big stick. And in that particular case Dewey and the American fleet represented the big stick. I asked on behalf of the nation the things to which we were entitled. I was as courteous as possible. I not only acted with justice, but with courtesy toward them. I put every battleship and every torpedo-boat on the sea under the American flag and Dewey, with instructions to hold himself ready in entire preparedness to sail at a moment's notice. That didn't mean that we were to have war. Dewey was the greatest possible provocation of peace."

It has been impossible for historians or biographers to agree how far to accept Roosevelt's 1916 account of the 1902 episode. The World War was raging, Roosevelt's hatred of the Germans had reached an almost hysterical de-

THE SECOND VENEZUELA CRISIS

gree of intensity, and there is little documentary evidence to support the story of the ultimatum. Certainly there was rising anti-German feeling in the country in 1902, and the Navy looked upon the Germans and not the British as the enemy, but the attitude of Roosevelt's administration was far less bellicose in 1902 than he seemed to indicate in 1916. There are no records of special orders to the fleet in the Navy Department. Undoubtedly there was anxiety in Washington over the anti-German feeling, and Roosevelt expressed himself strongly on German political activity in the Western Hemisphere. But beyond the verbal evidence there is nothing to prove that tension between the two countries had reached the point of an ultimatum. Roosevelt's restless and romantic temperament often led him to dramatize past events, and his superb self-confidence may easily have suggested to him that if he had considered it necessary to act in such a positive manner, his patriotism and daring would not have shirked the responsibility involved.

But unless, or until, further documentary evidence is forthcoming, one is compelled to accept the 1916 explanation with a certain amount of reservation.

Chapter XII

YANKEE IMPERIALISM

The Venezuela blockade had made it perfectly clear to Roosevelt that American opinion would not tolerate with any complacency a second debt-collecting expedition from European armed forces.[1] But such an attitude involved a number of disconcerting possibilities. The American Government " would certainly decline to go to war to prevent a foreign Government from collecting a just debt." But the question remained whether the occupation of customs houses for such collection would not very easily become a permanent one. The only escape from these alternatives, according to Roosevelt, " may at any time be that we must ourselves undertake to bring about some arrangement by which so much as possible of a just obligation shall be paid. It is far better that this country should put through such an arrangement rather than allow any foreign country to undertake it. . . . Moreover, for the United States to take such a position offers the only way of insuring us against a clash with a foreign power. The position is therefore

[1] See, for example, numbers of the *Literary Digest*, December 1902 and January 1903, with Press extracts from all the important newspapers.

YANKEE IMPERIALISM

in the interest of peace as well as in the interest of justice. It is of benefit to our people, it is of benefit to foreign peoples, and most of all it is really of benefit to the people of the country concerned."

Theodore Roosevelt developed his idea of the Doctrine to such a degree that it became the justification of his favourite policy, " Speak softly and carry a big stick, you will go far." During the next decade, 1903–13, Monroe's message, which was intended to be a warning *against* European intervention, was paradoxically paraded as a *justification* of United States intervention. In fact the Doctrine became a cloak for imperialism. The merits or demerits of imperialism do not concern this discussion, beyond the interesting fact that during a period of vigorous expansion the Doctrine still provided the key to foreign policy. By conveniently adding corollaries it was made to open any door in the expansionist policy of the administration.

On December 6, 1904, Roosevelt made the following statement :

" All that this country desires is to see the neighbouring countries stable, orderly and prosperous. Any country whose people conduct themselves well can count upon our hearty friendship. If a nation shows that it knows how to act with reasonable efficiency and decency in social and political matters, if it keeps order and pays its obligations, it need fear no interference from the United States. Chronic wrong-doing or an impotence which result in a general loosening of the ties of civilized society, may in America as elsewhere ultimately require intervention by some civilized nation, and in the Western Hemisphere the adherence of the United States to the Monroe Doctrine may force the United States, however reluctantly, in flagrant cases of such wrong-doing or impotence to the exercise of an international police power." [1]

When the question of intervention in San Domingo arose, Roosevelt wrote, " I have been hoping and praying for three months that the Santo Domingans would behave so that I would not have to act in any way. I want to do nothing but what a policeman has to do. . . . As for annexing the island I have about the same desire as a gorged boa constrictor might have to swallow a porcupine wrong-end-to. If I possibly can I want to do nothing to them. If it is absolutely necessary then I want to do as little as possible. Their government has been bedevilling us to establish some kind of protectorate over the islands and take charge of their finances. We have been answering them that we could not possibly go into the subject now at all."

But when rumours and dispatches began to reach Washington that certain political elements in the island were flirting with the idea of German control, the official attention became more alert and Roosevelt was coming to the conclusion that, " it was the duty of the United

[1] *Messages and Papers of the Presidents*, Vol. XVI., pp. 7053-54.

YANKEE IMPERIALISM

States to intervene in cases of brutal wrong-doing in the western hemisphere." [1]

" If," he concluded, " we are willing to let Germany or England act as the policeman of the Caribbean, then we can afford not to interfere when gross wrong-doing occurs. But if we intend to say Hands Off to the powers of Europe, sooner or later we must keep order ourselves." [2]

When Dominican affairs had reached a state of complete chaos Roosevelt acted according to his beliefs. The island was occupied for twenty-eight months. United States warships were sent to preserve order and prevent further revolution. The finances were stabilized, the foreign debt paid, and as far as the local government was concerned, the amount of revenue was greater than it had ever been in the past.

In more than one respect Roosevelt's foreign policy, and Taft's so-called dollar diplomacy which derived from it, is not without great merit, but it was unnecessary to shelter it behind the Doctrine.

Such a justification not only aroused distrust among Latin Americans, but to state, as Roosevelt stated, that it was " a part of that international duty which is necessarily involved in the assertion of the Monroe Doctrine," was unnecessarily to invite hostile criticism.

As far as the Doctrine is concerned it is open to the same criticism during the next thirty years. At one time or another during this period the

[1] To Elihu Root, May 20, 1904.
[2] To Elihu Root, June 7, 1904.

THE MONROE DOCTRINE AND WORLD PEACE

United States has concerned itself with the affairs of every Caribbean republic. This concern has expressed itself in various forms, from such extreme measures as occupation by American armed forces of San Dominico, Haiti, Nicaragua, Panama, and parts of Mexico to the precautionary step of sending warships to Cuba in 1933 " to protect if necessary the lives of American citizens pending the restoration of normal conditions of law and order." [1]

There is little doubt that when the Doctrine was invoked to justify these various acts it was a gross distortion of Monroe's original message, and must be referred not to 1823 but to 1904. For example, when Secretary of State Knox declared in 1912—" Whether rightfully or wrongly, we are in the eyes of the world and because of the Monroe Doctrine held responsible for the order of Central America and its proximity to the Canal Zone makes the preservation of peace in that neighbourhood particularly necessary "— he entirely confused the issue by dragging in the Doctrine.

Briefly, it can be said that Taft and Wilson continued Roosevelt's Latin American policy under the disguise of a distorted Doctrine.[2]

Wilson developed his idea of the Doctrine in his speech to Congress of December 2, 1913, exactly ninety years to the day after Monroe's message. The *New York World* remarked, " As

[1] *Washington Star*, August 20, 1933.
[2] There is such a vast amount of material concerning these recent events that there can be but a generalized and, I fear, very inadequate reference to them.

the Monroe Doctrine was aimed at the Holy Alliance so the Wilson doctrine is aimed at the professional revolutionists, the corrupting concessionaires and the corrupt dictators of all Latin America."

" It is a bold and radical doctrine." It was indeed. It was Roosevelt's big stick wrapped up in thick rolls of morality. It was the charter of the policeman, but a policeman with a different code of instructions.

Roosevelt and Wilson may seem at first glance to be poles apart in political ideas, but in practice, as far as Caribbean policy was concerned, the difference was superficial. Instead of resorting to the big stick Wilson invoked constitutionalism and tried to make it impossible for the Central American republics to indulge in their favourite political pastime of revolution. Nicaragua, the Dominican Republic, Haiti, Costa Rica, Cuba, and Panama all felt the heavy hand and the rolling periods of Wilson at one time or another. " Under the doctrine of constitutionalism he denied the right of revolution, not only to the five states of Central America but to all the rest of Latin America." [1]

This paternalism was resented quite as much as active coercion, in spite of Wilson's statement that the United States did not wish to acquire any more territory. His idea was to instruct the southern Republics how to govern themselves, with a fine disregard for the historical fact that petty dictators, financial chaos, *coup d'états*,

[1] Rippy, *America and the Strife of Europe.*

THE MONROE DOCTRINE AND WORLD PEACE

assassinations, and full-dress revolutions are or have been an integral part of Caribbean and Latin-American politics for more than a century. Wilson, in fact, had the laudable conception of " insistence on orderly constitutional democratic government " in countries where nice little upheavals are an important part of " natural rights." The fact that the United States had gained its own liberty by a bloody revolution is perhaps irrelevant, but there is no doubt whatever that Wilson used the Doctrine in the interests of American expansion no less than Roosevelt. Again, the merits of such a policy belong to a far wider discussion of foreign policy than this. Wilson's Caribbean policy, like his more important world policy, relied too much on lofty moral generalizations and too little upon political and psychological facts. He shut up his own greatness in a stubborn adherence to doctrines; he sent the Bible to the troops, but he forgot to give them any aeroplanes; he understood that " there can be no sense of safety and equality among the nations if great preponderating armaments are henceforth to continue here and there to be built up and maintained." But he did not conceive that half the world does not want equality and does want armaments, and thrives on a sense of danger. As far as the Doctrine itself is concerned, Wilson's most interesting reference to it is in his speech to the Senate on January 22, 1917.

" I am proposing, as it were," he explained, " that the nations should with one accord adopt the doctrine of President Monroe as the doctrine of the world : that no nation should seek to extend its policy over any other nation or people, but that every people should be left free to determine its own policy, its own way of development, unhindered, unthreatened, unafraid, the little along with the great and powerful.

" I am proposing that all nations henceforth avoid entangling alliances which would draw them into competitions of power, catch them in a net of intrigue and selfish rivalry, and disturb their own affairs with influences intruded from without. There is no entangling alliance in a concert of power."

This remarkable statement, delivered while Europe was pouring out the blood of its young men in a futile and agonizing death-struggle, reads to-day like a message from another world. The Monroe Doctrine was to become internationalized. A new world order based on self-determination was to take the place of power politics. But who was to enforce the Doctrine, against whom, and by what means, has not yet been determined to this day. The law of power, not the power of law, has hold of the peoples of the earth. Curiously enough, it is Washington, not Wilson, who supplies a guiding light at this juncture of events.

" We may choose peace or war as our interest guides, and justice shall counsel. Taking care always to keep ourselves by suitable establishments in a respectable defence position, we may

THE MONROE DOCTRINE AND WORLD PEACE

trust to temporary alliances for extraordinary emergencies."[1]

But perhaps the most interesting comment comes from Monroe himself. On January 1, 1917, the Assistant-Secretary of the Navy, Franklin D. Roosevelt, sent Wilson a letter enclosing an important document. In his letter the Secretary said, " I came across the enclosed memorandum while going over some papers, I acquired many years ago. It is in the handwriting of James Monroe, and was evidently written in 1814 when the Congress of Vienna was about to meet. I have been unable to discover that it was actually used in any official message or document ; but it is in many ways so interestingly parallel to events of the day that I thought you would like to add it to your collection of historical material."

The document of the President of 1814, sent to the President of 1917 by the President of 1937, contained the following sentences. " A war in Europe, to which Great Britain with her floating thunder, and other maritime powers are always parties, has long been found to spread its calamities into the remotest regions. Even the United States, just and pacific as their policy is, have not been able to avoid the alternative of either submitting to the most destructive and ignominious wrongs from European Belligerents, or of resisting them by an appeal to the sword : or to speak more properly, no other choice has been left to them but the time of making the appeal ;

[1] Inaugural Address.

it being evident that a submission too long protracted would have no other effect than to encourage and accumulate aggressions, until they should become altogether intolerable ; and until the loss of honour being added to other losses, redress by the sword itself would be rendered more slow and difficult."[1]

[1] Baker, *Woodrow Wilson, Life and Letters*, Vol. VI., p. 415*n*.

Chapter XIII

WHAT THE LAWYERS THINK

ADMITTEDLY the Monroe Doctrine is a political, not a legal manifesto. It is true that in other cases intervention has been exercised under pressure of public opinion—for example, Great Britain, France, and Russia intervened between Greece and Turkey in 1827. And we have seen that the question of American intervention on behalf of Greece had come up in Cabinet discussion four years before, when, in spite of great popular enthusiasm, it was wisely rejected by Adams as being contrary to American policy. Other cases, too numerous to mention, have occurred under one pretext or another, the last one being the late intervention of four Great Powers in the affairs of Spain under the careful scrutiny of the Non-intervention Committee.

" But whether there is really a rule of the law of nations which admits such interventions may well be doubted." [1]

The Covenant of the League of Nations attempted to legalize the position by providing for collective intervention to prevent any State

[1] Oppenheim, *International Law*, Vol. I., p. 255.

WHAT THE LAWYERS THINK

going to war or otherwise disturbing the peace of the world. The only difficulty encountered was that no State has been found which would put this admirable maxim into practice.

Many purists maintain that intervention is likewise admissible, or even has a basis of right, when exercised in the interests of humanity for the purpose of stopping religious persecution and endless cruelties in time of peace or war. Public opinion is certainly often in favour of such action, and it may perhaps be said that interventions in the interests of humanity are admissible provided they are exercised in the form of a collective intervention.[1]

Prophecy in politics, according to Lord Castlereagh, is a very idle occupation, although it is to-day one of the most overcrowded. Yet in discussing intervention it is not necessary to prophesy, but to emphasize the fact that the Doctrine contains no mention of United States intervention whatever. Far from being a policy of force, the Doctrine is a policy of protection. It will not come into conflict with the peace machine if that broken-down engine can be effectively started again, but it will certainly come into conflict with the war machine if that high-speed mechanism should appear as a menace to the country's vital interests.

Even a glance at the immediate past will show that the Doctrine has outlasted innumerable substitutes. We look forward to international elimination of force in relationships between

[1] Oppenheim, p. 255.

peoples. Instead of which we are confronted with a gigantic armaments race. We have heard of world co-operation and peace, but the world has grouped itself into conflicting ideologies. " Never since the Reformation have ideas been so freely discharged or so massively embodied ; but they have not yet been argued out, or fought out into any stable philosophy within which the nations may go their ways in peace." [1]

The idealistic agencies for a better world—the League of Nations, the World Court, the Kellog Pact—languish on the back pages of obscurity, or beg a penny from indignant patriots in one shirt or another. Not one of them possesses a single vestige of authority in the world to-day. On the other hand, the Doctrine has never died, in fact it may be said to have acquired more vigour to-day than it has had for a century. It can be argued that it is unfortunate that this is so, that America has sought to assert her rights as a World Power and has not accepted the corresponding responsibilities ; but the failure of the agencies for peace cannot be laid at America's door alone. The question of isolation will be examined by itself. It is necessary here to indicate the vitality of the Doctrine in the modern scene.

In 1912, when an American Company acquired land and harbour rights in Magdalena Bay on the coast of Mexico, and determined to sell their holdings to a Japanese company, they inquired of the State Department whether there was any

[1] G. M. Young in the *Sunday Times*, February 26, 1939.

WHAT THE LAWYERS THINK

objection. There was! The Senate adopted a resolution stating that the United States could not see the occupation or the possession of any harbour or other place on the American continents which could be used for military or naval purposes by any non-American Power without grave concern. This was orthodox Monroe Doctrine, and in view of the rise of the Totalitarian alliance and their known desire to secure a hold on South America, it is of some significance. The Tote Alliance is perfectly aware that "the European States are, as far as the Law of Nations is concerned, absolutely free to acquire territory in America as elsewhere."[1] And it is interesting to speculate upon what would have occurred had the Magdelena Bay Company told the Government to mind its own business and sold its holdings to the Japanese.

Other companies in English and American

[1] Oppenheim, *International Law*, Vol. I., p. 259.

This is most clearly illustrated by British reaction to the original message. During prolonged discussions between Rush for America and Stratford Canning and William Huskisson for England over the unsettled Oregon claims, Rush took his stand on the principles laid down by Monroe. After claiming all the territory about the Columbia River, he declared that " with respect to the whole of the remainder of that continent (North America) not actually occupied, the Powers of Europe were debarred from making new settlements, by the claim of the United States, as derived from their title from Spain."

To which the reply was that the British Plenipotentiaries asserted, in utter denial of the above principle, that they considered the unoccupied parts of America just as much open as heretofore to colonization by Great Britain as well as by any other European Powers, agreeably to the Convention of 1790 between the British and Spanish Governments, and that the United States would have no right whatever to take umbrage at the establishment of new colonies from Europe in any such parts of the American continent.

The British contention was certainly better law, but, as with all matters concerned with the Doctrine, politics, not law, is the determining factor.

history, John Company, for example, or the Standard Oil Company, have been able to pursue their policies for a considerable time in the face of Government opposition. But in this particular case it is probably safe to say that the Senate would have replied, this *is* our business, and would, moreover, have been able to summon overwhelming popular support had that been necessary. The " slogan-strength," is one more of the extra legal powers that the Doctrine has accumulated with the years.

It is true that some American writers claim that the Doctrine could be established as American International Law But this seems hardly tenable. President Wilson declared that it had never been formally accepted by any international agreement. " The Monroe Doctrine merely rests on the statement of the United States, that if certain things happen she will do certain things."

However, the fact remains that the Doctrine is still to be reckoned with as a fundamental principle in American foreign policy, and as yet it has never been seriously challenged [1] by any non-American Power. It is possible to make out a case that it has been violated—ten major violations according to M. Nerval, a bitter South American writer.[2]

But the case falls to the ground if the Doctrine is conceived as a national policy " enumerated so as to preserve the freedom of action of the United States." Thus interpreted it may be dia-

---

[1] France withdrew without fighting ; Britain temporized ; Germany ranted.   [2] Gaston Nerval, *Autopsy of the Monroe Doctrine*, chapter x.

WHAT THE LAWYERS THINK

bolical from M. Nerval's point of view, but its vitality as a national policy is unimpaired.[1]

It is important to point out that M. Nerval offers as a substitute a " new deal " in Pan-Americanism. The Doctrine is dead, he declares, but there is hope for the future in a true spirit of co-operation. In this he is at one with President Roosevelt's declarations and actions, all of which have aimed at just such a solution of South American problems.

The imperialism of the beginning of the century (when Cuba and the Philippines were annexed, the Panama Canal built, the " open door " in China filled with American traders) has given way to a policy of reducing commitments to a minimum. " The United States," writes Miss Ward,[2] " is neither decadent nor static but actively contractionist." One has the peculiar spectacle of the Philippino President journeying to Washington to suggest that it might be better if his island were *not* given full

[1] Tatum, *The United States and Europe, 1815-1823*, p. 296.
As a matter of fact there have been only five cases where violation of the Doctrine can be said to have occurred.
1. The seizure of the Falkland Islands by Great Britain in 1833.
2. The seizure of parts of Honduras by Great Britain shortly before 1860.
3. The intervention of France in Mexico during the American Civil War.
4. The re-occupation of the Dominican Republic by Spain, also during the Civil War.
5. The transfer of the island of St. Bartholomew from Sweden to France, 1877.
Only three of these five cases have remained to the present. The Falkland Islands, Honduras, and St. Bartholomew. Two or three other cases might possibly be added to this list according to the American historian, J. F. Rippy, but they are unimportant.
[2] Ward, *The International Share-out*, p. 9.

independence quite so soon as America had planned.

The same change of tone toward South America is remarkably well expressed by the Under-Secretary of State.

" I know," he said on July 20, 1937, "of no previous instance where the adoption by a Government of a new basis for its foreign policy has more rapidly produced concrete practical benefits than in the case of the adoption by the Government of the United States of the policy of the ' good neighbour ' in its relations with the other American republics. . . .

" By renouncing our earlier domineering rôle, by insisting upon the principle of judicial equality between all nations, and upon the inherent right of every sovereign people to be free from foreign interventions in its domestic concerns, we have not only helped to revitalize international morality : we have also gained friends."

This is undoubtedly true—but how does the Doctrine stand in relation to this enlightened policy ? Both Mr. Welles and President Roosevelt supply the answer.

"Any attempt," declares the Under-Secretary of State, "on the part of non-American Powers to exert through force their political or material influence on the American continent would be immediately a matter of the gravest concern not only to the United States, but to every other American republic as well, and appropriate action would undoubtedly at once be determined upon

WHAT THE LAWYERS THINK

as the result of common consultation between them."

Nor is President Roosevelt's declaration less significant. Before setting out to join the fleet in the most extensive manœuvres ever undertaken by the American Navy, he repeated what President Wilson had said, what other responsible men have said in the past—that America does not seek to acquire new territory anywhere, it desires to be on friendly terms with all nations whatever their form of Government may be; but, added the President, " representative Government in this hemisphere must and shall be maintained."

It is evident that there is remarkable harmony in the Government's South American policy, the main bases of which have not changed. The " new basis " that Mr. Welles speaks about could be better expressed as a new tone of voice. The words are much the same.

Chapter XIV

A LATIN-AMERICAN VIEWPOINT

But among the South Americans themselves there is no such harmony. General opposition to the Doctrine still exists, and there is, moreover, particular opposition to M. Nerval's Pan-Americanism. The Argentine, especially, feels itself strong enough to stand alone, and resents the paternal assumption of the over-lordship of a stronger Power.

Manuel Urgarte, a famous Latin-American publicist, in his book *The Destiny of a Continent*, makes this point of view quite clear.

"Those peoples," he writes, "which are destined to survive, group themselves together on a basis of racial kinship around the golden thread of an ideal of civilization. Our America, Spanish in its origin, is essentially Latin in its tendencies and inspirations. If it does not take a firm stand on its antecedents and its memories, whence is it to draw the necessary strength to preserve its personality, in spite of its disintegration and cosmopolitan character? A people which in developing is false to its race is a lost people.

"Our Latin America ought never to let herself

A LATIN-AMERICAN VIEWPOINT

be separated from Europe either in the economic order or from the cultural point of view ; for in Europe lies her only support in the conflicts which await her.

" The breakdown of Pan-Americanism in its present form is so obvious that even its most faithful adherents are vacillating. It was many years ago that the writer of this book denounced this political conception as a skilful move in the expansionist policy of the North, and a suicidal tendency of the simple-minded South."

Urgarte is admittedly a propagandist and uses exaggeration when he finds it expedient. The United States, he says, have done and will continue to do what all the strong peoples in history have done, and nothing can be more futile than the arguments used against this policy in Latin America. " To invoke ethics in international affairs is almost always a confession of defeat."

Among Urgarte's followers (and he has many) there are some who regret that the Spanish colonies ever revolted against Spain ; others suggest an imperial government of all Latin America to serve as a counter-balance to the United States. How preponderant the danger of Anglo-Saxon absorption appears to this Latin-American party is eloquently expressed by Urgarte himself and must be quoted in his own words ; though here again we must allow considerable leeway for the strong trade winds of a deeply felt racialism.

" Never," he writes, " in all history has such an irresistible or marvellously concerted force

THE MONROE DOCTRINE AND WORLD PEACE

been developed as that which the United States are bringing to bear upon the peoples which are geographically or politically within its reach in the Continent or on the shores of the sea. Rome applied uniform procedure. Spain persisted in a policy of ostentation and glittering show. Even in the present day England and France strive to dominate rather than absorb. Only the United States have understood how to modify the mechanism of expansion in accordance with the tendencies of the age, employing different tactics in each case, and shaking off the trammels of whatever may prove an impediment or a useless burden in the achievement of its aspirations. At times imperious, at other times suave, in certain cases apparently disinterested, in others implacable in its greed, pondering like a chess player who foresees every possible move, with a breadth of vision embracing many centuries, better informed and more resolute than any, without fits of passion, without forgetfulness, without fine sensibilities, without fear, carrying out a world activity in which everything is foreseen—North American imperialism is the most perfect instrument of domination which has been known throughout the ages." [1]

But the threat of this Yankee Peril, or whatever name we give it, is not all that Urgarte professes. South America as a whole has benefited rather than suffered from the existence of the Monroe Doctrine. It has been an open door policy and " it has saved South America from European

[1] Urgarte, *The Destiny of a Continent*, p. 125.

A LATIN-AMERICAN VIEWPOINT

domination and spheres of influence. And while the United States may as a result of the war have obtained a position of unexpected financial and commercial influence, England and Germany are recovering lost ground, and this rivalry will tremendously stimulate the delayed industrial development of one of the most wonderful regions in the world. . . . [1] With such an assured future these countries need have little fear of foreign domination."

The League of Nations gave the South American States a new view of their own importance, and opened a new chapter in the history of the Doctrine, but as that chapter appears at the moment to be suppressed by the censorship of the Totalitarian States, one may be permitted to cast some doubt upon the authoritative statement of Oppenheim that " with the growing strength of the Latin-American States the Doctrine will gradually disappear."

[1] Latané, *American Foreign Policy*, pp. 670–71.

Chapter XV

THE DOCTRINE IS NO MENACE

In a peaceful world devoted to trade, commerce, and the pursuit of the arts of civilization and humanity no doubt all policies of a defensive as well as an aggressive nature would die quietly while mankind enjoyed the fruits of peace and prosperity. But we live in a very different world indeed—a world of armed peace surrounded with secret plans and overhung with suspicion and hysteria, which can promise us little more than a highwayman's paradise where we are strong enough to confront him with his own weapons. Under such conditions it is unlikely that the Monroe Doctrine will disappear, though that is no reason to assume that it is a threat or a menace to any South American State.

Consider for a moment the age of the millennium that we missed, as embodied in the proposed Treaty for the Renunciation of War in 1928. When the United States invited Great Britain to become a party to this treaty, the British reply contained the following sensible passage which is little more than the declaration of a British Monroe Doctrine although the exact sphere is not defined.

THE DOCTRINE IS NO MENACE

"There are certain regions of the world the welfare and integrity of which constitute a special and vital interest for our peace and safety. His Majesty's Government have been at pains to make it clear in the past that interference with these regions cannot be suffered. Their protection against attack is to the British Empire a measure of self-defence. It must be clearly understood that His Majesty's Government in Great Britain accept the new treaty upon the distinct understanding that it does not prejudice their freedom of action in this respect. The Government of the United States have comparable interests, any disregard of which by a foreign Power they have declared that they would regard as an unfriendly act." [1]

This is, if not a formal, at least a tacit admission by Britain of the right of the United States to exercise the Doctrine, and the United States could not do otherwise than admit the right of Britain as expressed in the reply just quoted.[2]

---

[1] Quoted by Oppenheim, *International Law*, Vol. I., p. 260n.

[2] However, it is instructive to notice that neither the United States nor Great Britain are prepared to accept Japan's claim to an Eastern Monroe Doctrine. Both Powers deny her right " to make conclusive its will in situations where there are involved the rights, the obligations and the legitimate interests of other sovereign states." The Japanese contention cannot be taken as parallel, as Japan would like to make it appear, since the attack on China can scarcely be accepted as a measure of Japanese defence, or the slaughter of hundreds of thousands of Chinese be interpreted as " a special and vital interest to the peace and safety of Japan." In this connection it is interesting to hear the Japanese explanation and the American reply. In January 1936 the Japanese Ambassador at Washington, M. Saito, explained his country's policy in the following terms :

" Up to the time of the World War all the great nations of the West

THE MONROE DOCTRINE AND WORLD PEACE

But it would be untrue to regard those certain regions of the world mentioned in the British note as being menaced by Britain and it is equally untrue to regard the American Doctrine as a menace to any South American State. When Elihu Root declared that the Monroe Doctrine does not assert, or imply, or involve any right on the part of the United States to impair or control the independent sovereignty of any American State—he was repeating in different words the formula that Adams arrived at when he prepared to answer Canning and Alexander I.

When Mr. Welles, the American Under-Secretary of State, spoke on foreign policy in February 1939, he made it perfectly clear that Fascist penetration in the United States or in Latin America would be resented and resisted. He declared that the American people and their Government " possess and will avail themselves of the right to protest against—or if need be, to challenge—the foreign policy of any other nations

---

possessed territory in East Asia which they had taken from the Chinese or other people near to Japan. These Occidental aggressions had caused the Japanese to wage several minor wars and at least one major war. Naturally our people want no repetition of these Western encroachments into their sphere of the world. The United States would countenance favourably none in any part of the Americas from Europe or Asia."

This attempt to point a parallel between Japanese policy toward China on the one hand and the policy of the Monroe Doctrine toward Latin America on the other is not convincing. It was effectively disposed of by Senator Pittman, Chairman of the Senate Foreign Relations Committee, when he said in Congress, " We are seeking to preserve the republics of Latin America, not to destroy them." He added that the authentic Monroe Doctrine for China was the Nine Power Treaty in which the leading nations, including Japan, had guaranteed her territorial and political integrity.—*U.S. in World Affairs*, 1936, p. 66.

THE DOCTRINE IS NO MENACE

which threaten the peace or security of the United States."

Such an attitude by no means implied, as Mr. Welles pointed out, that the United States had a right to assail or condemn the form of government under which other people lived, however divergent from its own.

" We desire to maintain friendly relations with all people," he said. " We do not presume to suggest by what form of government other peoples should be ruled.

" But to the degree that a foreign Government persists in policies of inhumanity or refuses to respect the treaty rights and legitimate interests of this country, or its national policy threatens our security, friendship and understanding between the United States and that Government must be correspondingly impaired."

The Doctrine in fact has returned to its original basis.

Chapter XVI

THE CASE FOR ISOLATION

The chief diplomatic aim of Adams and Monroe was isolation from Europe ; immunity from the endless wars, alliances, and intrigues of that remote continent. It was not an easy business. But it was understood by the people, it was no enigma, it was a popular expression, and it can be summed up briefly in the report of a speech in Congress by a Mr. Trimble of Ohio delivered on March 28, 1822.

" All civilized nations," he said, " were under the dominion of two great social systems, differing widely from each other—that one was established in the Occidental, the other in the Oriental world—that the spirit of the age was against the European system. It [the American system] has two aspects, two essential principles—one political the other commercial. The first is known and distinguished by written constitutions, representative government, religious toleration, freedom of opinion, of speech, and of the press. The second by sailors' rights, free trade, and freedom of the seas. Contrast it with the European system. The political character of that system is aristocracy, monarchy, imperial government, arbitrary

THE CASE FOR ISOLATION

power, passive obedience, and unconditional submission. Its commercial character is prohibition, restriction, interdiction, empressment, colonial monopoly and maritime domination." [1]

The case for isolation, therefore, rested on a distinct and demonstrable difference of system, commercial and political. But there were other implications equally important. The United States was not yet a Great Power, but she was ambitious and exuberant. In order to expand she must be left alone. The enormous and uncalculated territory on her western frontier was hers by a natural and inevitable destiny, only if she could hope to manœuvre in such a way that she would not find herself suddenly confronted by one of the Great Powers and consequently be forced to accept the European system of alliances on the American continent in order to exist. The Doctrine was the embodiment of this hope and the protector of this ambition.

More than a century has passed since the famous message was given to the world. The great experiment in democracy has been proved to be one of the two most stable governments in the world.

And in England, the only other and older example, both the form and practice of government have felt the recoil of " the one successful democratic revolution." No other Great Power to-day—neither France, Germany, Italy, nor Russia—has preserved a traditional form of government for a century.

[1] *Annals of Congress.* 17 Congress 1, Session House, March 28, 1822.

THE MONROE DOCTRINE AND WORLD PEACE

Jefferson, Adams, and Monroe, following Washington's lead, emphasized America's need for isolation and detachment as sources of strength—and so they have proved to be beyond the most miraculous hopes.

But America no longer occupies " the detached and distant situation " which Washington contemplated with such satisfaction. A policy of political isolation, the very thought of which will draw long and deplorable sentences from Opposition Senators, is no longer in tune with political realism. The world has shrunk, Europe is not a remote continent, England is far from being the most powerful nation. The internal-combustion engine, radio, aeroplanes, and a hundred other inventions have altered the physical world and social intercourse beyond the wildest conception of the Fathers. Whether this is a change for the better or not is another matter. But no one can help but admire the men who dared to form a Doctrine for their own protection, so effectively that it still works under conditions which are completely different.

To many Americans the post-war confusion in Europe has appeared not less precarious than the Europe of 1823 did to Monroe and his Cabinet, and the case for isolation has been revived with all its old allurement.

This modern case for isolation is a curious matter, and the fact that recent events have revealed that its foundations, like the foundations of St. Mark's, are built on piles which have decayed with age does not appear to disturb its

THE CASE FOR ISOLATION

architects. But there is something ambiguous about it which when examined reveals a characteristic profoundly out of touch with the national character. It is in fact " the attitude of the Levite who pulled his skirts together and passed by on the other side."

Moreover, this attitude is justified, according to Mr. Quincy Howe in his famous book, *England Expects Every American to do His Duty*, by a desperate appeal to, of all things, fear of England's diplomacy. In order to escape this terrible menace, Mr. Howe has suggested a policy of extreme isolation. It is obvious to him that co-operation is a waste of time since England has everything to gain and America everything to lose. Mr. Howe's book appeared in 1937, that is to say, four years after Germany's gigantic effort at rearmament, when the first fruits of that hideous sowing were being reaped in abundance. Events have moved rapidly since then and American policy has gone through some interesting changes. The fascination of Mr. Howe's thesis has somewhat wilted as it becomes more apparent than ever that humanity is all in the same boat. But it is still worth examining as the best and most widely read example of the American theory of isolation.

America must withdraw from the concert of nations, she must beware lest Britain beckon her into a new war. Britain, according to Mr. Howe, is working with subtle and insidious propaganda to make America underwrite the Empire. So obsessed with this idea is Mr. Howe that he

THE MONROE DOCTRINE AND WORLD PEACE

suggests that England has been responsible for the Monroe Doctrine—the Open Door—American entry into the Great War—the Washington Naval Conference—and the rise and fall of the League of Nations.[1] It is doubtless very flattering to the British, but it is a curiously distorted and inaccurate rendering of England's policy toward America, or for that matter of America's foreign policy from Monroe to Roosevelt. "It could have been said just as neatly and just as truly that for a hundred years every American had expected England to do *his* duty—if there be any duty put upon mankind to maintain the régime of law in a world anarchic by nature."[2]

Mr. Howe represents America as being devoid of men capable of being the guardians of her safety or the mouthpieces of her greatness. Faced with her ancient rival she appears to him to be helpless, uninstructed, naïve; there is but one escape, let her isolate herself with self-sufficiency. How can this be done? The isolationists reply: America must give no protection to American property, American lives, or American shipping in any war zone, wherever it may be. (This, one supposes, must be left to the British.) Nor in the event of war should America lend any money or provide any war materials to any one. "The present Neutrality Act should therefore be repealed at once and a mandatory measure substituted. This should contain no

---

[1] Howe, *England Expects Every American to do His Duty*, pp. 17, 20, 30, etc.
[2] *The U.S. in World Affairs*, 1937, p. 38.

THE CASE FOR ISOLATION

cash-and-carry clause and should forbid all trade with any warring power." [1]

America should tell its citizens quite firmly that they should not take sides, that there is never any right in any fight, even a fight for life is wrong; that America is in the world but not of it, or if she is, she is quite unable to manage her own affairs as long as British diplomacy exists in the same world. Therefore she should withdraw into her own self-sufficiency, and presumably issue moral bulletins of her interesting condition. She can, declares Mr. Howe, " promote western civilization by preserving it in the one country where it has not gone into a decline." But to promote this wonderful thing she must immediately get rid of all her overseas possessions by giving them complete independence so that she will have no responsibility for their defence. She must then sit down upon her own shores clutching the charter of her self-sufficiency and prostrating herself in pious horror while the Japanese or the Germans, the Italians, the Russians, or even the wicked English dispute the complete independence of the various islands and territories in their own decadent and disgusting way, without anything to stop them more remarkable than an American note.

She should apologize to the Japanese for her traditional policy of the open door (this being a British invention), and in future prevent her ships and 'planes from going out of sight, or, at least, very far from the American coast. In fact

[1] Howe, *op. cit.*, p. 216.

THE MONROE DOCTRINE AND WORLD PEACE

she should adopt an obsequious neutrality which would allow her to be kicked off the seven seas, because she has a great big continent of her own to play about with where she can lay the foundations of self-sufficiency. And if, following an ancient longing, she should still build ships they should be nice small ships so that every one, particularly the British, who have great big ships, will see that they could not possibly sail very far from the shore.[1]

It is an interesting prospect to contemplate. It savours of that inordinate desire for Utopianism which is the sublime form of self-deceit, and leaves mere sordid realism, one supposes, to the sinister and mysterious workings of British diplomacy.

The fact is that Mr. Howe and the isolationists want neutrality at any price, and are willing to commit America on any question of an abstract character so long as it appears to answer that hypothetical state of affairs. There is but one answer to such a thesis. When actual danger menaces the interests or the system of the country, the reply will be not theoretical but practical; in the meantime America " cannot and will not commit herself upon abstract and speculative principles of precaution."

When Monroe and Adams formulated the Doctrine they did not mean to enunciate maxims

---

[1] Ships should be forbidden from steaming *for any reason whatever*, except on an errand of mercy, more than 500 miles from the American coast.

The planes are given another 250 miles leeway before they should be required to turn tail.

Mr. Howe quotes General Butler with approbation, *op. cit.*, p. 206.

THE CASE FOR ISOLATION

of foreign policy for many years to come. " They were thinking of an immediate danger. The language of the original Doctrine was directed toward an existing situation." [1]

On the other hand the framers of the twenty-two neutrality Acts which appeared in Congress from time to time during 1936 and 1937 were trying to build a " Chinese wall on the Atlantic and Pacific coasts to shut out the sounds of bombardment, invective and ideological screechings." Yet at the very outset they were made to look ridiculous by a naturalized American citizen of Latvian origin, by occupation a dealer in junk, who conceived the idea of shipping old aeroplanes to the Government forces in Spain. Not having dealt with civil wars in their Bills the neutrality gentlemen were forced to pass a special law for Spain while the enterprising junk dealer loaded his cargo in haste. The ship put to sea a few hours before the Bill took effect, but although she had evaded neutrality she fell into the hands of the insurgents, and was a total loss.

So-called " permanent neutrality laws " dealing with imaginary contingencies will undoubtedly defeat themselves. Their real purpose is to minimize provocative incidents before they occur. But in practice they will inevitably limit the freedom of action of the elected government and embarrass every attempt to deal realistically with complicated, shifting, and critical situations. Their permanence cannot be expected to survive even one serious crisis when national

[1] Perkins, *The Monroe Doctrine, op. cit.*, p. 260.

THE MONROE DOCTRINE AND WORLD PEACE

interests are being trampled on, and President Roosevelt himself has given the opinion that they increase rather than decrease international tension and, consequently, the likelihood of trouble for America. So it would appear that the case for isolation has come full cycle.

Adams and Monroe believed implicitly in the right of peoples to determine the form of their government. "They made no attempt to force any particular form on the States of the New World, at no time exerted more than a moral influence in favour of republicanism, they were really, in their own day, the champions of principles of liberty."[1] But they would have looked with scepticism at any law which attempted to limit their freedom of action in some indefinite future. It could only seem to be a denial of free government by the people themselves; an attempt, in fact, to lock and bolt the stable door, not after the horse had escaped, but even before they had a horse to keep in the stable.

[1] Perkins, *op. cit.*, p. 259.

Chapter XVII

THEN AND NOW

THE isolationists point to Washington's farewell address of 1796 as the sacred corner-stone of their policy. But it is important to observe that Washington was not establishing a precedent, he was expressing ideas that were both current and familiar. Moreover, he himself had made an alliance with a European Power without which it is unlikely that he could have encouraged his countrymen not to do likewise. As a cautious statesman he was dealing with the immediate problems with a realistic and positive policy. " Europe," he declared, " has a set of primary interests which to us have none, or a very remote relation. Hence she must be engaged in frequent controversies, the causes of which are essentially foreign to our concerns. Hence, therefore, it must be unwise in us to implicate ourselves by artificial ties in the ordinary vicissitudes of her politics or the ordinary combinations and collisions of her friendships or enmities."

Thus, at the beginning of her history as a nation, America was forced to pursue a policy of expediency in forming an alliance with France, although the men who were responsible

THE MONROE DOCTRINE AND WORLD PEACE

for it were firmly convinced that it could not become a *permanent* part of her foreign policy. They knew that neither allies nor enemies wished to see America rise to power. They understood Europe well enough to realize that the Powers would do everything possible to involve her in their own endless and sanguinary disputes over the Balance of Power, and they saw quite clearly and rightly that the true road to power and empire lay in a policy of isolation. The Doctrine was a logical development of the same desire and the same ambition. It enlarged the sphere of isolation, it met the real or imaginary threats of those who differed in political outlook, and it preserved vast territories for the imperial spirit that lived on equal terms with republican philosophy.

America has never had to uphold the Monroe Doctrine by force of arms. Up until the present she has been able to regulate the conduct and the transactions of European Powers in South and Central America by peaceful influence or diplomatic persuasion. However, there is little doubt that she would back up persuasion by force if she felt her national security was menaced. The violations of the Doctrine have been discussed already. Is it probable that other attempts will be made? There have been extravagant predictions by newspapers and journals and wild surmises of the schemes of the dictators in South America. We are told that the new alliance of the Totalitarian States is infinitely stronger than the Holy Alliance, and the added

THEN AND NOW

peril of Japan in the Pacific makes the American continents vulnerable on both coasts. But before being stampeded down byways of disaster it must be observed that hitherto the confusion of politics and the diversion of wars in Europe have acted as a protection to America. Unless there were a combined attack by Germany, Italy, and Japan on the Panama Canal or some supposedly weak strategic point on the American continents, it is difficult to believe that any real danger exists so long as the American Navy commands the seas around both continents. But consider even such an event as a combined attack. It would mean that Italy would abandon the Mediterranean, Germany the Baltic, and Japan the China Sea, in order to risk battle with the American Fleet and Air Force operating in home waters. It assumes that France and England keep their ships in port and take no advantage of such tremendous lines of communication to adjust a new European Balance of Power. It assumes that the inhabitants of Central or South America would not resist such an incursion, even if it were possible to effect a landing.

But dismissing such a course of events as improbable, it remains a fact that the new conflict of ideologies in Europe has already had definite repercussions in the South American States. Alien groups of Italians and Germans have been able to play an important part in politics, and the ideas of the dictators have made considerable headway. The Council for Foreign Relations estimates that the Italian element in the Argentine and Brazil forms one-third of the population, and is Fascist in sympathy.

The German elements, though not so numerous, preserve close " cultural relations " with the Nazi régime, and radio propaganda from Berlin has been added to newspapers and lectures as a means of keeping a direct hold over the population.

Could this introduction of foreign ideas become a serious menace ? Suppose one or more of the republics in the South should adopt, of their own accord, a totalitarian government, and seek direct military aid from Europe ? What if the Rome-Berlin axis should decide to ship warplanes and munitions to support a revolt to the extreme Right in one of the States? Have they not acted in precisely the same way in Spain ? Would the Doctrine be invoked to prevent such interference ? These questions which ardent and sensational journalists are shouting from headlines, have been answered in part by various moves of the State Department. President Roosevelt's trip to South America in the autumn of 1936, his speeches and the proposals of his Secretary of State, Mr. Cordell Hull, were not merely an ingenuous attempt to point out to a disturbed Europe the blessings of American civilization. Behind the cheering and the sunshine talk lay a direct warning to both Continents against subtle attacks upon their constitutional government. There was also an important reference to the Doctrine itself, for President Roosevelt implied that the unilateral character of the

THEN AND NOW

policy which Latin America has always bitterly resented has given way to a policy of mutual consultation in the event of a crisis.

There are, of course, more recent developments which clearly indicate that Washington is alive to the importance of South American independence of Europe. The repeal of the neutrality law is being urged by the administration, and American naval shipyards have been authorized to supply armaments to South American States.

In his extremely enlightening declaration to the Senate Foreign Relations Committee on April 5, 1939, Mr. Stimson, a former Secretary of State, remarked that " we had only to look to the South of us to realize that even we are in the zone of their [the Axis] orbit."

And on the following day the *Times* disclosed a startling piece of news, doubtless already known in Washington. It is worth recalling at the risk of being charged with sensationalism, for it indicates the vast scale on which power politics is being conducted to-day. In March 1939 Herr Adolf Mueller, acting head of the Nazi organization in Argentina, was arrested and charged with engaging in subversive activities. He was accused of having signed a report on plans for a German annexation of Patagonia in the South of the Argentine. The region possesses oil wells, and is of great strategic importance because it dominates the Straits of Magellan, the only route except the Panama Canal from the Atlantic to the Pacific. A German or Japanese squadron based securely in South America within striking

THE MONROE DOCTRINE AND WORLD PEACE

distance of the South Atlantic and Pacific trade routes would without doubt constitute a challenge to the Doctrine which would not be regarded " without grave concern " by the guardians of the Panama Canal.

In general, it can be said that a dangerous violation is highly improbable, and should it occur, the United States is more than able to deal with it. But America's strategic position in the world, her stupendous resources, and her proved interest in world order and peace give the Doctrine a peculiar importance in world affairs.

As long as the present trend of power politics prevails in Europe, the peace of the world will depend as hitherto on defensive alliances formed by those who desire to retain their possessions against those who desire to increase theirs.[1]

Ultimately it may be the reign of the extremists will give way—either to the gigantic delirium of a new world conflict which will sweep them into it, or to the impatience of the moderate and predominating factors in human nature which may insist upon turning that corner in human progress which will put militarism behind it forever—only then will the famous Doctrine lie quietly in the archives of history. But the time is not yet.

NOTE.—It must be emphasized that the Monroe Doctrine is but one part of American foreign policy concerned with certain measures considered necessary to the interests and security

[1] Balfour Memorandum, 1916.

of the country. It is probable that these interests will become more important than ever, although there is no particular reason to refer to the Doctrine to justify them. Certainly in the past it has been unwise to try to force other aspects of foreign policy, other causes for intervention, and other necessities for expansion into the limitations of the doctrine. Control and direction of national power may have nothing whatever to do with the Monroe Doctrine and yet be vital elements in American foreign policy.

CHAPTER XVIII

AFTER MUNICH

THERE is no doubt whatever that the Munich crisis,[1] the rape of Czechoslovakia,[2] the Lithuanian ultimatum,[3] and in all likelihood a procession of further crises, have helped to reorientate American foreign policy. The solid basis of the isolationists appears suddenly to be built upon sand. The keystone of the Doctrine has been knocked out and the whole building threatens to collapse—for the Doctrine " asserts the right of sovereignty and self-protection upon which international law is based, and it states the conditions which would endanger this international right as far as the United States is concerned."

Sovereignty, self-protection, and international right have been ruthlessly trampled upon. A vast Empire of ninety million people, moulded into a military machine, dominates the Continent and imposes its will and its fantastic rhythm upon all Europe. There is no reason to suppose it will stop of its own accord. During the Munich crisis it possessed a striking power greater than any possible alliance; it is hypnotized by a leader

[1] September 1938.   [2] March 1939.   [3] March 1939.

AFTER MUNICH

whose declared ambition is to extend his influence over Europe, and whose ultimate goal appears to be that which has led the war lords of all history to destruction—the domination of the world by force.

It is a curious occurrence that a series of bloodless victories has been the means of changing the world outlook as it has not been changed since Napoleon's campaign in Italy. It deserves a closer examination. By using the new threat of air attack—a threat which was of minor importance during the Great War—Germany gained everything she had set out to gain. Aggressive imperialism appeared in a new guise of National Socialism. The State, not the capitalist, became the exploiter of the individual. Intellectual independence gave way to mass suggestion, spiritual pride was taught the goose-step, civilization was found to rest on the uncomfortable points of bayonets. The world in fact became less interesting because it became cruder. The really exciting adventures of the human mind and spirit gave way, or threaten to give way, to the rough divisions of political ideologies, to the menace of air attack, and the diversion of a huge increase of human energy into the creation of the machinery of death. Under the barrier of unreason we are being forced into a kind of party politics, to our own impoverishment.

America has become acutely, almost passionately, interested in world affairs—from a complacent security she has started awake to find that crises in Europe have a very definite effect

THE MONROE DOCTRINE AND WORLD PEACE

upon her own interests. The intricacies of the former European diplomacy, from which Jefferson once remarked that he wished America were separated by a sea of fire, have given way to something much simpler and much more terrifying. Well-turned phrases of understatement backed by small professional expeditionary forces are things of the past. Moreover, the moral issues in international relations are no longer treated with that circumspection which endowed them with a pleasant complacency. They are no longer treated at all. Germany and Italy proclaim with a crude clarity that would have profoundly shocked the old imperialists, that they intend to establish their empires, and they have proceeded to do so. Conquest is not merely for economic power, but for the satisfaction of a dream of Roman Empire or the mystical conception of a ruling Aryan race. All the most unpleasant qualities of human character have been erected into ideals for the edification of youth : insensitiveness to cruelty ; infantile adoration of the weapons of slaughter ; egoism and violence. Everything, in fact, is twisted by politics.

The reaction of America to the Munich settlement has been definite and outspoken. A rearmament programme has been proposed and passed with the declared intention of making the Western Hemisphere safe from European attack. This may be said to be orthodox Monroe Doctrine, but there are other considerations. Many thoughtful people believe that a devastating

AFTER MUNICH

attack on France and England by the Totalitarian States would mean that America would at once be involved. Mr. Hoover's statement in February [1] that if the dictators began dropping bombs on London and Paris, "Washington could not be restrained from action," is significant of the change, the very natural change, in American feeling. Mr. Hoover is a former President, a Republican leader, and a declared isolationist. But the controversy on isolation has changed with the change in world politics.

Lord Lothian, in a leading article on America's position after Munich, wrote in February 1939:

" Behind the general question of the possibility of the United States being drawn into a world war there is an increasing recognition that America's own vital interests are being profoundly affected by the rise in the strength of the Totalitarian Powers and the relative decline in the power of Great Britain and France. For instance, while Mr. Hull's visit to Lima was more successful than has generally been thought in convincing the leaders of the South American Republics that they have a common interest in resisting either political or economic aggression from Europe or Asia, there is still widespread anxiety in the United States about German and Italian penetration into South America and of the consequent threat to the Monroe Doctrine. For instance, the establishment of Italy and Germany in a controlling position in Spain and still more in Portugal and their African and insular posses-

[1] 1939.

sions would constitute as formidable a threat to the Monroe Doctrine and the power of the United States to enforce it as to British communications with the East."

But the question is larger than any threat to South America could constitute. Under pressure of public opinion the Monroe Doctrine, in fact, may assume once more something of a Wilsonian aspect. It is useless for the isolationists to hide their heads in the sand. They may doubt America's importance in the world, they may proclaim she has no rights, no interests and no business outside latitude this and longitude that. They may even believe their own declarations—but no one else does. In more than one sense America occupies, and will occupy, a world position analogous to that of Great Britain at the time of Monroe's message. " This will not be because she now aspires to any such position. Quite the contrary, her desire is still for isolation without responsibility. But it will be forced upon her, as it was forced upon us mainly against our will." [1]

At the time of Monroe's message England refused to commit herself either to the Holy Alliance on the one hand or to concerted action with America on the other. In other words, she insisted on maintaining a policy of isolation and strength. The Alliance could be used if it suited her plans; if not, she was strong enough to follow her own policy at her own leisure.

There is less leisure in the world to-day:

[1] Lord Lothian in the *Observer*, February 26, 1939.

AFTER MUNICH

there is an understandable tendency to cling to any tradition or formula which appears to stand against anarchy. The life of the famous Doctrine has been prolonged and enlarged far beyond the dreams of those who created it. It has been called upon to justify complete American control of the Panama Canal ; it has been invoked with passionate insistence to settle the boundary dispute between Britain and Venezuela. It has been used with most unfortunate results to draw the effective strength out of the League of Nations. It has had the strength and weakness of an adored article of faith. It has become, by eternal repetition, " one of those habitual maxims which are no longer reasoned upon but felt." [1]

Under Theodore Roosevelt it was transformed from a Doctrine intended for the protection of the States of the New World against intervention from Europe into a doctrine of intervention by the United States. Under Franklin Roosevelt it has returned to the protective basis upon which it was founded.

There was never a time in our national history, according to the Secretary of State, when the influence of the United States was more urgently needed than at present—to serve both our own best interests and those of the entire human race.

" The search for national isolation springs from the council of despair.

" Not through a sudden and craven abandonment of our national traditions, nor through attempts to turn our backs upon our responsi-

[1] Crampton, British Minister in Washington, May 1848.

THE MONROE DOCTRINE AND WORLD PEACE

bilities as a member of the family of civilized nations can we advance and promote the best interests of our people.

" It is my firm conviction that national isolation is not a means to security but rather a fruitful source of insecurity. For while we may seek to withdraw from participation in world affairs, we cannot thereby withdraw from the world itself." [1]

There are two courses open to us. Either we will continue to pour a tremendous, an overwhelming amount of human energy into the manufacture of the machinery of death, or we will have to adopt a reasonable form of a new League of Nations which will survive to become the United States of the World, as the thirteen sovereign states survived to become the United States of America. At present Unreason is in the saddle, and none of us can afford to remain weak unless we are willing to be trampled underfoot with relentless and scornful brutality. Justice without strength is futile, and if we believe in the justice of our laws and institutions we must be strong as we have never been strong before. And on that strength we must rebuild an international order and restore respect for international engagements ; we must bring it home to those Powers who worship force, that force must be controlled and directed, that aggression does not pay. For if we cannot do this, then assuredly the day is not far off when we will be involved in the ruin of the civilization of our time.

[1] Cordell Hull, June 3, 1938, quoted by Rippy, *America and the Strife of Europe*, p. 232.

APPENDIX

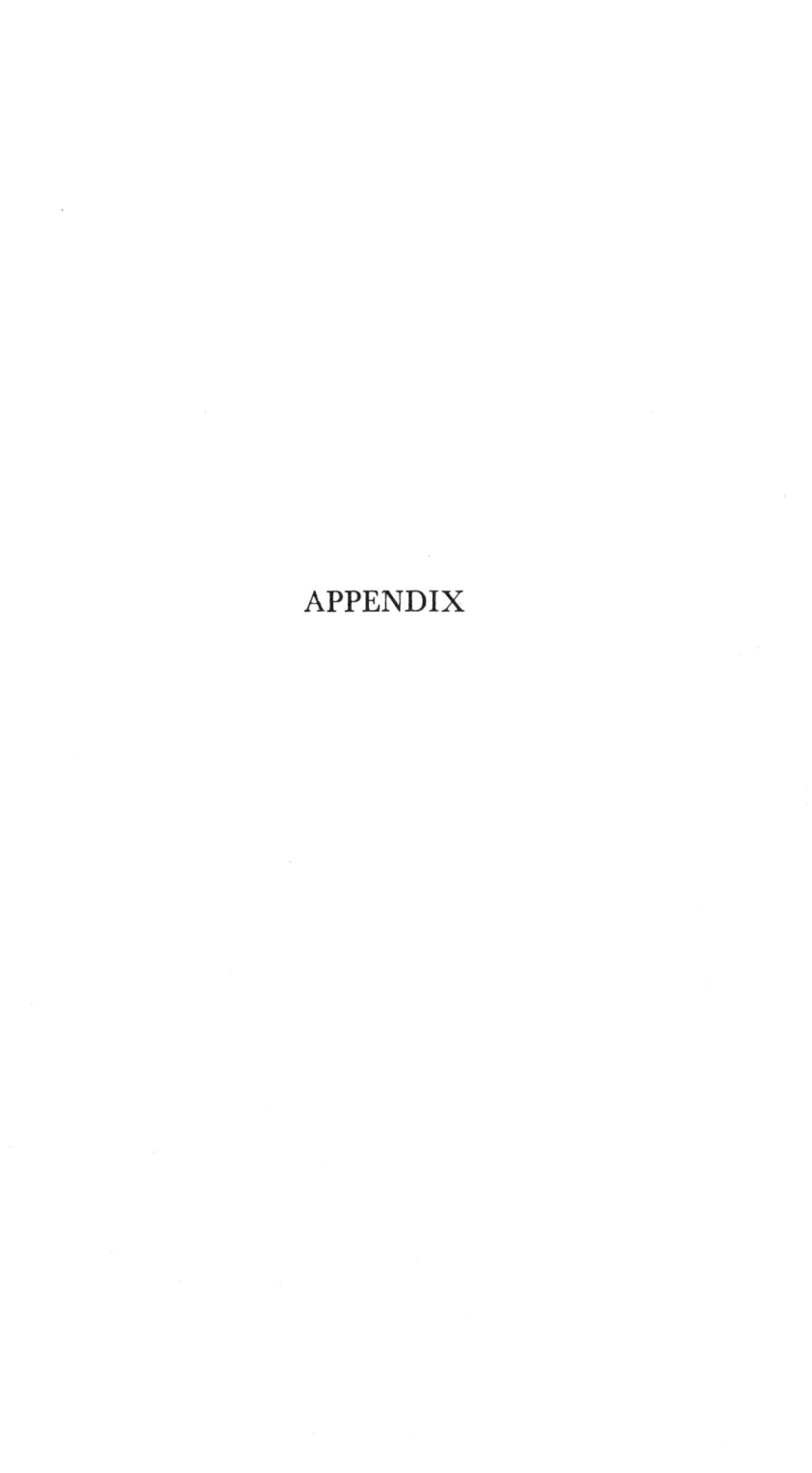

APPENDIX

The Pan-American Conference, 1938
Press Review

Dec. 2, 1938. En route for Lima. Secretary of State Cordell Hull and the American Delegation to the Pan-American Conference observed to-day the 115th anniversary of the Monroe Doctrine which may receive a new interpretation at the Lima meeting. That interpretation may carry the Doctrine a step further to link all the States of the Western Hemisphere against any aggression from without, instead of letting the burden rest solely on the shoulders of the United States.

Secretary Hull has been concerned over new methods by which the Totalitarian States already have gained a foothold in South America : intensive political propaganda and artificial systems of trade.

In such words the *New York Times* correspondent described the beginning of the 8th Pan-American Conference at Lima. The " new methods " are of course not in the least new. Political propaganda and artificial systems of trade have existed since time immemorial. But the use of them by Italy and Germany to pene-

APPENDIX

trate South American markets formerly controlled by London and New York is a disturbing factor which cast its shadow over the historic meeting. And since the Doctrine is concerned with foreign control in the Western Hemisphere some account of the meeting at Lima may help to indicate how intricate and vast the game of power politics has become. Almost every one of the following reports comes from a different source. Yet they form an astonishingly vivid picture of one event.

Dec. 5. Lima. There has recently been a heavy influx of German and Italian unofficial " observers."

Germany has appointed a new and much more aggressive Minister here on the eve of the conference. The Nazi leader here has just cut short a vacation in Germany to get back before the conference opens.

Several medical and archæological professors have arrived, ostensibly to lecture on their specialities. Actually they are devoting their energies to attacking Pan-Americanism.

The Italian Legation staff, already over-manned, has been further increased.

Typical of anti-American propaganda was a scathing attack on Pan-Americanism and President Roosevelt's bugbear of German invasion of South America by Professor Ubbelolide-Doering of Munich at San Marcos University.

It would be foolish to pretend that the Rome-Berlin axis is not exerting a strong influence on the forthcoming conference.

APPENDIX

Dec. 7. It is expected that quiet efforts will be made to persuade Latin-American countries to dispense with their British, German, Italian and other European military advisers and missions in favour of United States experts.

Dec. 7. Mexico City. The newspaper *Universal* warns Latin America to be equally wary of European Fascist nations and of the United States—both, it is claimed, seek economic and political domination of weaker nations of Latin America.

Dec. 10. Totalitarian observers and propagandists are attacking the United States. In other days European agents in Latin America attacked the Monroe Doctrine. To-day the process is repeated.

Dec. 12. Caustic comments from Japan. According to a Tokyo paper the United States is planning to obtain hegemony over American countries and develop them into a military alliance. Under the pretext of the menace of Fascism the United States is planning to make her own economic invasion, which is the main object of her dollar diplomacy, hitherto attempted under cover of the Monroe Doctrine.

Dec. 14. Rio de Janeiro. Germany and Italy are continuing in radio broadcasts and press dispatches printed here to attack the United States as the Lima Conference progresses. They issue warnings that Yankee imperialism is motivated by mercenary economic considerations.

Dec. 14. Lima. Five German correspondents stalked out of a committee session to-day to show

APPENDIX

their displeasure over a speech attacking Germany.

The incident occurred when Dantes Bellegarde of Haiti declared that the Americas could not possibly have anything in common with a nation that had reverted to customs of the Middle Ages and had set man against man, race against race, and class against class.

Dec. 15. Mexico. In the name of democracy and freedom of commerce no attempt must be made to prevent Mexico's obtaining Japanese beans, German machinery, and Italian silks. Even less can we turn our back on European culture under the slogan of combating political systems that do not suit us.

Frankly we should not trust the United States.

Dec. 16. Washington. In the diplomatic corps of Washington there is no surprise over the news from Lima that Argentina and other Latin-American nations are unwilling to go as far textually as the United States wants them to go in the message aimed at Berlin, Rome, and Tokyo.

"Yet," concludes Arthur Krock, "the background is interesting and revealing as proof that despite the arbitrary allocation of geography that divides the world into an Eastern and Western hemisphere (instead of Northern and Southern) the interests of all the nations in the Americas are by the testimony of our own official acts not necessarily akin."

Dec. 18. Buenos Aires. Hundreds of boys of high school and college ages have set themselves

APPENDIX

the task of arousing Argentina's 12,000,000 people to the perils of Yankee imperialism.

Their placards warn Argentina that President Roosevelt's good-neighbour policy is a " farce " and a blind. Despite police banns they attempt to hold meetings in the broad squares of Buenos Aires.

Dec. 19. Lima. With only six working days left, the 8th Pan-American Conference was confronted to-day with the task of taking action on 150 projects, in addition to working out a compromise between the divergent viewpoints of Argentina and the United States on the keynote problem of continental solidarity.

Dec. 21. Argentina rejects Solidarity Draft.

. . . Unable to alter her position opposing any sweeping declaration of Pan-American solidarity in the face of extra American aggression.

From John White, *New York Times* special correspondent at Lima :

"There seems to be every indication that the United States will come out of the 8th Pan-American Conference with less prestige than at any time in the last ten years. With only three more working days it is difficult to see how the situation can be saved before adjournment.

"The Totalitarian States have made an issue of this conference and put democracy on the defensive."

New York Times leading article the same day :

At this moment the real danger to the solidarity of the American nations is not an external but

APPENDIX

an internal danger. It lurks in the possibility that strong minority groups of German or Italian or Japanese in some of the South American countries will attempt to form a state within a state.

Dec. 22. Berlin. Nazi newspapers described conference moves to weld the American republics in a defensive unit as " United States failure Number 1." They called the whole conference a failure, and condemned what they called Roosevelt's imperialism and his " Jewish controlled government."

Dec. 25. Twenty-one American republics sign pact to resist aggression.

"The 8th Pan-American Conference crowned its labours to-day with unanimous announcement that the republics of the Western Hemisphere intend to make common cause in the face of a threat of force."

This Declaration of Lima, according to John White, "is a compromise draft drawn up to conciliate twenty-one conflicting viewpoints. The declaration was arrived at by the democratic process in open discussion in open convention. It may go down to history as the greatest international achievement of the democratic process to date."

Dec. 28. Lima. A German broadcast in South America last night viciously attacked the conference as a failure because of difference of opinions.

Throughout the conference the Nazi and Fascist reporters have maintained a haughty

APPENDIX

attitude of disapproval of the entire proceedings. Not only did they flood South America as well as their home papers with distorted reports of the proceedings and bitter attacks on the conference's aims, but at conference meetings they openly showed their disapproval of what was going on.

Dec. 28. Washington. President Roosevelt declared that he considered the Pan-American Conference a great success.

Paris. A new League of Nations is born in America.

Berlin. Roosevelt in close collaboration with certain Jewish banks of New York for years has been pursuing a policy of conquering South America with dollars. In Lima, however, Roosevelt had bad luck.

The stronger Spain becomes in Europe, the stronger the Spanish element in South America asserts itself, the more the South Americans strive to conduct their policies and business on their own merits and the weaker becomes Roosevelt's position at home.

Dec. 29. Washington. Arthur Krock commending the Secretary of State Mr. Cordell Hull: " The average politician would shun the risks of a Pan-American conference. Differences among the Latin-American republics—the so-called republics—and the North American democracy are as basic and wise as if some of these countries were stationed in the moon. The Western Hemisphere is in some respects a geographical myth. The political philosophy which is the

APPENDIX

dearest possession of this government does not fit the ideas or wishes of many of the statesmen who gathered at the conference. But Mr. Hull patiently and constantly returns, quietly but firmly continuing to preach his theme : the political and economic inter-dependence of a rather ill-assorted group of people. Trouble doesn't trouble him, but he certainly knows how to trouble trouble."

Thus the conference came to a close. John White, the *New York Times* correspondent, made sensational disclosures about dictatorial censorship during the session and wrote that on the opening day Lima had "appeared to be the site of a great Nazi rally rather than the site of a Pan-American Conference. Thousands of Italian and swastika flags had filled the streets to the exclusion of the flags of the nations taking part in the meeting."

And Mr. Hull, in an interview on board ship on his return, expressed strongly his opinion "that Europe was headed for a terrific smash up unless some new influence, not now in sight, appeared on the scene, and that the United States and the other American countries will suffer intensely even if not directly involved."

The reporter also discovered that although the conference had been successful, general official opinion appeared to be that Congress would now concern itself with a revision of the Neutrality Act and an armament programme. And when questioned later about Mr. White's story Mr. Hull declared with "considerable emphasis"

APPENDIX

that he had no idea of allowing the valuable and significant features of the international gathering to degenerate into a bitter sensational squabble.

My thanks are due to the courtesy and consideration of the *New York Times* London Office in allowing me to examine their files and indices.

INDEX

Aberdeen, George Gordon, fourth Earl of, 72, 74.
Adams, John Quincy, 122 ; and Monroe, 10, 56, 64–65, 138, 140, 144, 146 ; and England, 17, 29, 44, 45, 56 *et seq.*, 136 ; and Russia, 26 *et seq.*, 51 *et seq.*, 136 ; *Memoirs* of, quoted, 31, 32, 35, 36, 53, 57–58, 60, 62 ; on transfer of Cuba, 35–36, 53 ; isolation aim of, 138, 140.
Addington, Henry, Viscount Sidmouth, letter of, to Canning, 66–67.
Alaskan Boundary Tribunal, quoted, 30.
Alexander I., Tsar, 19–20, 20–21, 27 *et seq.*, 51, 58, 136:
America and the Strife of Europe (Rippy), 117, 160.
American Foreign Policy (Latané), cited, 72*n*, 77, 87, 131, 133.
American Historical Review (Ford), quoted, 31–32, 38, 62, 66.
American Historical Society (Hart), quoted, 12.
Americans in England (Mowat), quoted, 25–26.
Annals of Congress, quoted, 138–39.
Argentine, 149–50, 151, 165.
Austria, 101 ; and the Mexican adventure, 82–83.
Autopsy of the Monroe Doctrine (Nerval), cited, 126.

Balfour, A. J., first Earl of, 100*n*, 101, 107, 152*n*.
Bayard, Thomas, 96.
Behring, Vitus, 26–27.
Belize, 70.
Bellegarde, Dantes, 164.
Blaine, James G., 89.

Brazil, 46, 70, 150.
Britain, 11, 114, 122, 132, 139, 157 ; and the Monroe Doctrine, 15 *et seq.*, 63, 66–67, 69 *et seq.*, 91 *et seq.*, 125*n*, 135, 142 ; and colonization in the New World, 15 *et seq.*, 28, 70 *et seq.* ; the enemy of U.S.A., 15–16, 18, 22 *et seq.* ; and Cuba, 16, 33 *et seq.*, 46, 49, 53, 55 ; and the Holy Alliance, 17, 33, 41, 43, 53, 92 ; and the Balance of Power, 21, 29 ; naval power of, 22, 27, 47 ; and South America, 36 *et seq.*, 44 *et seq.*, 51 *et seq.* ; and the Mexican adventure, 81, 82 ; and the Panama Canal, 87 *et seq.* ; and the Venezuela question, 91 *et seq.* ; and Japan, 135*n* ; and American isolation, 140 *et seq.*, 157 *et seq.*
British and Foreign State Papers, quoted, 105.
British Guiana, dispute concerning boundary of, 91 *et seq.*
Buchanan, President James, 80.
Buenos Aires, 164–65.
Bulwer, Sir Henry, 87.

California, 53, 71, 73, 74, 75, 77, 82.
Cambridge History of British Foreign Policy, quoted, 16, 46.
Canning (Petrie), quoted, 47.
Canning, Stratford, 32, 34, 66, 125*n*, 136 ; and the Monroe Doctrine, 16, 69 ; and South America, 36 *et seq.*, 44–50, 51 *et seq.*
Castlereagh, Robert Stewart, Viscount, 23, 34, 123.
Chamberlain, Joseph, 98, 101.

INDEX

Chamberlain, Sir Austen, 107.
Chili, 53.
China, 127, 135*n*.
Civil War, American, 80, 82, 83, 84-85, 127*n*.
Clayton-Bulwer Treaty (1850), 87, 89-90.
Cleveland, President Grover, and the Venezuela crises, 93, 96 *et seq*.
Colonial Policy of Great Britain (?), quoted, 25.
Columbia Treaty (1846), 87.
Convention of London (1861), 81.
Costa Rica, 117.
Cranborne, Robert Arthur, Viscount, 107.
Cuba, 19, 116 ; England and, 16, 33 *et seq.*, 46, 49, 53, 55 ; annexation of, by America, 102, 127.
Cushing, Caleb, 70.
Czartoryski, Prince (*Memoirs*), quoted, 21.
Czechoslovakia, 154.

Daily Telegraph, cited, 12-13.
Devonshire, Spencer Cavendish, eighth Duke of, 107.
Dewey, Admiral George, 109, 110.
Dictionary American Bibliography (Perkins), quoted, 64.
Dominican Republic, 103, 115, 117, 127*n*.
Dwight, Reverend Timothy, 19 *and n*.

England. *See* Britain.
England Expects Every American to do His Duty (Howe), 9*n* ; cited, 16, 108, 141, 142-43, 144.

Falkland Islands, 70, 71, 127*n*.
Fish, Hamilton, 86.
Florida, 34.
Foreign Policy of Canning (Temperley), quoted, 38, 45, 46-47.
France, 29, 33, 41, 48, 53, 57, 65, 69, 72 *and n*, 73, 77, 122, 126*n*, 127*n*, 139, 147 ; and South America, 44-45 ; on the Monroe Doctrine, 76 ; and the Mexican adventure, 80 *et seq*.
Franklin, Benjamin, 9*n*.

Germany, 12, 115, 126*n*, 133, 139, 149 ; in conflict with the Monroe Doctrine, 90, 100, 102-3 ; and the second Venezuela Crisis, 103 *et seq*. *See also* Totalitarian States.
Ghent, Treaty of, 18, 25-32.
Granville, George Leveson-Gower, second Earl of, 89.
Great Britain and the United States (Mowat), quoted, 49.
Great War, 142, 155.
Greece, 65, 122.
Grover Cleveland (Nevins), cited, 90.
Guizot, Prime Minister, 76.

Hague Tribunal, 106.
Haiti, 103, 116, 117.
Hansard, quoted, 99, 106.
Harcourt, Sir William, 98.
Hay, John, 89, 103.
Hayes, President Rutherford, 88.
Histoire Parlementaire de France, quoted, 73.
Holy Alliance, 27-28, 33, 41, 53, 55, 56, 58, 65, 117, 148, 158.
Honduras, 127*n*.
Hoover, President Herbert, 157.
Howe, Quincy, on isolation, 141-144.
Hull, Cordell, 59, 150, 157, 160, 161, 167, 168-69.
Huskisson, William, 125*n*.

International Law (Oppenheim), cited, 122, 123, 125, 135.
Irving, Washington, 25-26.
Italy, 139, 149. *See also* Totalitarian States.

Jameson Raid, 100.
Japan, 68, 135*n*, 148, 163.
Jefferson, President Thomas, 35, 54, 55-56, 66, 140, 156.
Johnson, H., 12-13.

INDEX

Kellog Pact, 124.
Kipling, Rudyard, 106-7.
Knox, Philander C., 116.
Krock, Arthur, 164, 167.

La Doctrine de Monroe (De Baumarchais), cited, 102.
Lansdowne, Henry William, sixth Marquis, 105, 107.
Latin America. *See* South America.
League of Nations, 122, 124, 133, 142, 159.
Les États-Unis et la doctrine de Monroe (Pétin), cited, 102.
Lima, 157, 161 *et seq.*
Lincoln, President Abraham, 83.
Literary Digest, 112n.
Lithuania, 154.
Lodge, Henry Cabot, 93, 103.
Lothian, Philip Henry, eleventh Marquis of, quoted, 10n, 17, 157-58.

McKinley, President William, 101.
Madison, President James, 54.
Magdalena Bay Company, 125.
Mahan, Admiral Alfred T., 107-8.
Massachusetts Historical Society (Ford), quoted, 61, 64, 65.
Maximilian and Charlotte of Mexico (Corti), 85n.
Maximilian, Emperor of Mexico (Archduke Ferdinand Maximilian of Austria), 81 *et seq.*
Mexico, 46, 48, 53, 69 *et seq.*, 74, 77, 116, 124, 127n; Maximilian, Emperor of, 78-85; and the Totalitarian States, 164.
Miles' Weekly Register, 19n.
Monroe, President James, 9, 10, 35, 49, 56, 89, 100n, 119, 144, 146; dispatches of, to Rush, 38 *et seq.*; position of, 64-68; isolation aim of, 138, 140.
Morning Chronicle, cited, 76.
Mueller, Adolf, 151.
Munich crisis, 154 *et seq.*

Narrowing World (Roosevelt), 10, 12.

National Review, 108.
National Socialism, 155.
Navigation Laws, 60.
Nerval, Gaston, 126, 127.
Neutrality Act, 142, 168.
New York Times, 169; cited, 68, 161, 165-66, 168.
New York World, quoted, 98, 116-17.
Nicaragua, 87, 116.
Niles Weekly Register, quoted, 25.
Nine Power Treaty, 136n.
North American Review, quoted, 93.

Observer, quoted, 10n, 11-12, 157-158.
Olney, Richard, 75, 89, 91, 93 *et seq.*
Oregon, 71, 73, 75, 77, 125n.

Pakenham, Richard, 71, 74.
Palmerston, Henry John, third Viscount, 72.
Panama, 116, 117.
— Canal, 68, 86-90, 127, 149, 151, 152, 159.
— Congress of, 49.
Pan-Americanism, 127, 130, 131, 161 *et seq.*
Patagonia, 151.
Pauncefote, Julian, Baron, 89.
Peru, 53.
Philippines, 102, 127.
Polk, President James K., 73, 75, 76, 77.
Portugal, 157.

Remarks (Dwight), cited, 19.
Review of Reviews, 108.
Rio de Janeiro, 163.
Rivalry between U.S. and Great Britain over Latin America (Rippy) quoted, 16, 47.
Roosevelt, President Franklin, 120; on the "narrowing world," 10, 12; on interference in the American continent, 128-129; on neutrality laws, 146; and South America, 150, 162, 165, 166, 167; Monroe Doctrine under, 159.

INDEX

Roosevelt, President Theodore, 93, 105, 100, 112 *et seq.* ; and Monroe Doctrine, 103, 113, 159 ; and Germany, 109-11.
Root, Elihu, 103, 136.
Rush, Richard, 16, 32, 51 *et seq.*, 58, 59, 61, 125*n* : *Court of London*, quoted, 36-37 ; dispatches of, 33-43.
Russia, 15, 16, 17, 26 *et seq.*, 52, 53, 57, 66, 122, 139. *See also* Alexander, Tsar.

St. Bartholomew, island, 86, 127*n*.
St. James's Gazette, quoted, 97.
Salisbury, Robert Arthur, third Marquis of, 96, 98, 99, 100.
Samoa, 102.
San Domingo, 114.
Schomburgk, Sir Robert, 91.
Seward, William H., 83-84, 85.
Sketch Book, 19*n*.
South America, 33 *et seq.*, 52, 53, 56, 61, 67, 69, 125, 128-29, 130-33, 136 and *n*, 148 *et seq.*
— American States. *See* South America.
Spain, 14, 15, 33 *et seq.*, 41, 53, 65, 69, 80, 100, 103, 122, 131, 145, 159, 167.
Star, cited, 45-46.
Stimson, Henry L., 151.
Sunday Times, quoted, 124.
Sweden, 86, 127*n*.

Taft, President Howard, 115, 116.
Texas, 71, 72 and *n*, 73, 75, 76-77.
The Destiny of a Continent (Urgarte), quoted, 130-31, 131-32.
The Edinburgh Review, 19*n*.
The International Share-out (Ward), 60*n*, 127.
The Monroe Doctrine (Perkins), quoted, 27, 30, 59-60, 62, 69, 75, 91, 145, 146.
The National Intelligence, 19*n*.
The North-American Review, 19*n*.
The Pamphleteer, 19*n*.
The Quarterly Review, 19*n*, 25-26.
The United States and Europe (Tatum), quoted, 10-11, 20-21, 22-23, 34, 63, 127.
The United States and Mexico (Rippy), 85*n*.
The U.S. in World Affairs, quoted, 11, 136*n*, 142.
Times, 107 ; quoted, 76, 151.
Totalitarian States, 125, 133, 154 *et seq.*, 148 *et seq.*
Tuyll, Baron de, 31, 52.

Ubbelolide-Doering, Professor, 162.
Universal, newspaper, 163.
Urgarte, Manuel, quoted, 130-31, 131-32.

Venezuela, 86, 89, 159 ; first crisis over, 90, 91-100 ; second crisis over, 90, 101-11.
Vera Cruz, 70.
Verona, Congress of, 33, 34.
Vienna, Congress of, 21, 22, 120.

Wake, island, 102.
Washington Naval Conference, 142.
Washington, President George, 119, 140, 147.
Washington Star, quoted, 116.
Welles, Sumner, quoted, 128, 129, 136-37.
West Indian Islands, 86, 103.
White, John, 165, 166, 168.
Wilson, President Woodrow, 116, 117, 118-20, 129.
Woodrow Wilson (Baker), quoted, 120, 121.
World Court, 124.

Young, G. M., quoted, 124.